THE
HEART of DAVID
JOURNAL

Leading with Vision, Passion, and Wisdom.

VOLUME 2

by David Mayorga

Published by

SHABAR PUBLICATIONS
McALLEN, TEXAS

Most Shabar Publications products are available at special quantity discounts for bulk purchase for sales promotions, fund-raising and educational needs. For details, write Shabar Publications at mayorga1126@gmail.com.

The Heart of David Journal Volume 2
Leading with Vision, Passion, and Wisdom
by David Mayorga

Published by Shabar Publications
3833 N. Taylor Rd.
Palmhurst, Texas 78573
www.shabarpublications.com

ISBN: 978-0-999171-05-9

Contents

1

The Season of His Visitation!

"And they will level you to the ground, and your children within you, and will not leave a stone upon a stone within you, because you did not know the season of your visitation." (Luke 19:44 Berean Literal Bible)

In my devotion today, I want to take you back in time to the days of Jesus during His earthly life. Most of us are familiar with the story of Jesus Christ being sent from heaven by the Father and how He offered His life as a ransom for all.

The Lord visited His people, but not everyone recognized His visit. In fact, many hated Him, saw Him as a false prophet; others thought demons possessed him, and so on. Still, some believed in Him and followed Him wholeheartedly.

The image I share with you illustrates the ongoing awareness of God's presence within and around you. It's safe to say that our beliefs are values that shape our lives. Furthermore, the choices we make, rooted in these beliefs and values, are what truly define us and often influence our actions.

The visitation of Jesus Christ and His coming into the world was no accident; His visitation truly offered a door of opportunity for anyone willing to see it that way. People were scattered like sheep without a shepherd. We can be sheep under a shepherd's care, or we can be sheep scattered without guidance. This decision is entirely up to you.

As you go through life, engage in ministry, or run a business for God, it is wise to recognize God's ongoing visitation in your life. When the Lord visits you personally, it is solely to guide you regarding your destiny in

Him. Ignoring this fact would shortchange your life and almost everything you hope to achieve.

Don't go another day without recognizing His visitation in your life. What does a visitation look like?

- A visitation is a sense that God is moving old things (mindsets, traditions, and/or comfort zones) around to make room for the new.
- A visitation also brings a sense of dissatisfaction within you and around you. Reason: God no longer wants you to be comfortable in your current state. He wants you to understand what He is doing or about to do in you and through you.
- A visitation triggers feelings of anger in you. Reason: God wants you to recognize your old way of living and compare it to His new heavenly pattern. The goal is to align your heart with His.

People today live mindless and spiritless lives. This is clear from the confusion surrounding everyone, including believers. The daily experience of visitation is an excellent opportunity you can begin to embrace. In fact, I don't believe you can stay sane, peaceful, and full of joy in this world anymore without experiencing God each day! Neh'enah.

2

The Abishai Syndrome –
A Lesson on Character-Building and Brokenness

"So, David arose and came to the place where Saul had encamped. And David saw the place where Saul lay, and Abner the son of Ner, the commander of his army. Now Saul lay within the camp, with the people encamped all around him. Then David answered, and said to Ahimelech the Hittite and to Abishai the son of Zeruiah, brother of Joab, saying, "Who will go down with me to Saul in the camp?" And Abishai said, "I will go down with you." So, David and Abishai came to the people by night; and there Saul lay sleeping within the camp, with his spear stuck in the ground by his head. And Abner and the people lay all around him. Then Abishai said to David, "God has delivered your enemy into your hand this day. Now therefore, please, let me strike him at once with the spear, right to the earth; and I will not have to strike him a second time!" But David said to Abishai, "Do not destroy him; for who can stretch out his hand against the Lord's anointed, and be guiltless?" David said furthermore, "As the Lord lives, the Lord shall strike him, or his day shall come to die, or he shall go out to battle and perish. The Lord forbid that I should stretch out my hand against the Lord's anointed. But please, take now the spear and the jug of water that are by his head, and let us go." So, David took the spear and the jug of water by Saul's head, and they got away; and no man saw or knew it or awoke. For they were all asleep, because a deep sleep from the Lord had fallen on them." (1 Samuel 26:5-12)

Today, I share with you one of the most profound lessons on brokenness—a lesson that molds your character deep into your spirit.

If you have studied or read about the life of little David before he became the king of Israel, you will see how God anointed him from his youth and how the Lord's hand empowered him multiple times.

David was profoundly anointed as a true worshipper, brave warrior, and powerful king. His spirit was united with God, his soul was committed to fighting for the name of Jehovah, and his body demonstrated the ability to lead with passion and wisdom as one of the most fabulous kings ever to walk this planet.

Along with the precious gifts of God upon David's life, his followers' praise was loudly expressed in the streets. Now, King Saul was good, but David was great! The people danced and sang, "Saul slains thousands, but David his tens of thousands!" This popular song reached King Saul's ears, and he became very upset, jealous, and envious of David. This marked the beginning of a much different level of testing for David, and he would experience the brokenness God intended for his promotion.

Scholars say that King Saul attempted to kill David more than twenty-three times!

Once, while David was fleeing to save his life from King Saul, he found that King Saul and his army were sleeping in a nearby camp. David asked some of his men to go with him to find out where Saul was camping. Abishai decided to join David and assess the situation. To their surprise, they found King Saul asleep, along with his commander Abner, and a sword stuck in the ground next to Saul's head.

When Abishai saw this situation, he quickly seized the opportunity and told David: **"God has delivered your enemy into your hand today. Now therefore, please, let me strike him at once with the spear, right to the ground; and I will not have to strike him a second time!"** Abishai responded to the moment, but he never once asked the Lord or even considered what God intended to do in testing David's character.

David, a man of prayer and devotion to God, reacted differently. Listen to David's heart as he responds to Abishai: **"David said to Abishai, "Do not destroy him; for who can stretch out his hand against the Lord's anointed, and be guiltless?" David said furthermore, "As the Lord lives, the Lord shall strike him, or his day shall come to die, or he shall go out to battle and perish. The Lord forbid that I should stretch out my hand against the Lord's anointed."**

David faced a difficult decision. He could have acted on the twenty-three times Saul tried to kill him and justified revenge. He could have said, "God made this happen so I could put this wicked king out of his misery!" He could have easily killed the older king and taken the throne, since David was not afraid to use his sword. But David chose neither option: he didn't listen to his hurt, his emotions, or his fellow soldier Abishai; he only listened to his conscience, which was God's conscience.

In Abishai's view, David missed a great opportunity to get revenge on the man who wanted to kill him. You see, Abishai was a man with an unwavering spirit. He saw the chance to advance himself. David saw it as an opportunity to grow in God.

Abishai saw the sword lying on the ground next to Saul's head, noticed the deep sleep they were in, and thought, "This is it, David! God has made it possible for you to kill this man! For crying out loud, David – let me take his head off!" David replied, "No. God will deal with him later."

Now, listen to this one line of Scripture at the very end of this story: **"For they were all asleep, because a deep sleep from the Lord had fallen on them."** Do you see the setup? God arranged this entire situation to see what David would do with the opportunity at hand.

It was God who caused a heavy sleep to fall on Saul and his army so He could see where David's heart truly was.

My friends, be mindful of this in your own lives. Leadership is not about opportunities simply appearing, but about God's purpose! It's not about what we desire or wish for but about sensing our heavenly Father's guidance. It's not about what I want or when I want it but about obeying the pattern of God that has been engraved in our hearts. Neh'enah.

3

If Not Now, Then When?
Overcoming Laziness & Procrastination

While meditating during my quiet time, I reflected on a passage of Scripture that spoke to my heart. Let me share some of the principles I discovered that might also impact your life. Here's what the Proverb of King Solomon says: **"I passed by a lazy person's field and by the vineyard of someone with no sense. Thorns had grown up everywhere. The ground was covered with weeds, and the stoned walls had fallen down. I thought about what I had seen; I learned this lesson from what I saw. You sleep a little; you take a nap. You fold your hands and lie down to rest. Soon you will be as poor as if you had been robbed; You will have as little as if you had been held up."** (Proverbs 24:30-34)

Without offending anyone, I encourage you to take an honest look at your own life and evaluate your current situation. Have there been times when something on your agenda wasn't completed? Have you ever made plans to start a project but never "got around to it"? Maybe you did begin the project and made some progress but never finished it. Are you someone who starts quickly but struggles to finish? Are there many unfinished tasks on your "things to do" list? If so, just remember that you're not alone! We've all been in this place before, and I must say, more than once.

How does someone end up in disgrace, broke, and feeling "ripped off" by life altogether? There is a reason for this happening in a person's life. All these things don't just happen by chance or because they are having a bad day or a case of "bad luck."

Most of life's misfortunes stem from practicing habits that lead us astray. If someone adopts principles that promote victory and success, they will enjoy a prosperous life and future; however, if a person practices laziness and procrastination throughout their life and neglects the necessary efforts for success, they will end up in poverty.

The personal philosophy you create in overcoming laziness and procrastination will greatly influence your life. Let me outline some powerful philosophical ideas that can help us defeat laziness and procrastination.

1. Never prioritize the urgent over the important! Once you've written down your goals and started your project, don't stray from it. I'm sure that "emergencies" will come up, but don't focus on them. Stick to the important items on your list and stay the course!

2. Do It While the Fire Is Burning! When an idea comes to you, act on it immediately! Don't delay for another day. The perfect time to start is the moment the vision or desire strikes you! The key is to do it when the passion of inspiration is alive! Procrastinating only makes it harder to accomplish, and eventually, the passion fades along with the dream. Should have, could have, but didn't!

3. Procrastination Is Costly! If you don't deal with the problem while it's still manageable, it could end up being very expensive. Ignoring something that's broken when you know it's broken might make it impossible to repair. Don't wait another day. For example, imagine a leaky roof. If you don't fix it, each rain will cause more damage through rust and corrosion. Over time, practicing this bad habit could lead to your roof collapsing! That will be costly, and you'll wish you had acted sooner.

It's clear that the Proverb highlights the rewards and consequences for a lazy man. All decline begins with neglect. It doesn't require a major act of carelessness. It all starts with a "little." A little here, a little there, and eventually, poverty will follow.

Remember the words, **"You sleep a little; you take a nap. You fold your**

hands and lie down to rest. Soon you will be as poor as if you had been robbed; you will have as little as if you had been held up."

My prayer is that all this benefits you in some small or significant way! Always keep this instruction in mind! Neh'enah.

4

Why Maybe the Way You Think, Talk, and Act Are Holding Back Your Future!

"For as he thinks in his heart, so is he." (Proverbs 23:7a)

As I sat at the coffee shop on a beautiful early morning this past week, a comment made by one person to another caught my attention. The comment was "If there is a will, there is a way!" Have you heard this comment before? It's not the first time I have heard it, but it was the first time I questioned it. Is that comment true? Does it really work? Why would anyone say something like that? What about those who have a strong will to accomplish something but don't? I had all these thoughts going through my mind, and I concluded: "If there is a will, there is a way!" True, but only partially.

Let me share my insights from my journey toward excellence. The longer I live, the more I realize that vision is much more powerful than "will-power." Vision can lead me to my goals in ways that human willpower alone cannot. I've tried human "will" before; it got me started, but it didn't have the strength to carry me all the way through.

While watching television, you will notice constant infomercials advertising exercise machines, health gimmicks, and similar products. The infomercials often feature people sharing their testimonials about how effective and beneficial they have found these products. They tend to exaggerate by claiming that using a particular machine or trying dietary supplements has led to significant breakthroughs.

Many people fall for this and try to get the newest machine on the market or a dietary supplement. After weeks of using a new machine, they get tired of minimal results and eventually give up. How do I know this? It has happened to many people I know personally, including myself. What went wrong? Was it effort? Was it a lack of "willpower"? All these questions run through our minds as we try to understand why we can't lose the extra weight.

Here's what I've learned after recently losing 14 lbs. I realized that to succeed in anything you do, you must have a vision for it. Losing weight is no different. Opening a business is no different. Starting a new project is no different. You need to see the pure, the good, the great, and the beautiful. Visualize the finished product before taking the first step! Positive projection is essential for anything to manifest.

Too often, we hear people jokingly say, "I hope this thing works out." Others say, "I'm not sure about doing this, but I hope to God I can lose all this weight." My friends, you have sealed your fate with this kind of language. Your comments reveal a lack of vision. This way of speaking will not get the job done!

You must see what you want to become! You need to keep visualizing what you want to achieve! If you don't do this, you won't reach your goal, and your vision will never come true.

The key to survival in any venture is optimistic projection! You need to keep visualizing your destination to ensure your vision endures. Always keep the end goal in mind. For example, you might look at your exercise program and realize that after a whole month of working out hard, you've only lost two pounds. This can be discouraging!

Keep in mind who you want to be in twelve months. In business, if your sales decline in the first quarter, review the finished product and let it guide you by inspiring better strategy and techniques if you want to stay competitive in your market.

With positive outlook, everything is possible! Without it, failure becomes unavoidable. Remember, before you begin, take a good look at the finished product, then continue with a positive outlook until you cross the finish line. Someone said, "If you can see it, you can do it!" I believe this. Neh'enah.

5

Through Faith & Patience
You Will Inherit Your Promise!

"Better is the end of a thing than the beginning of it, and the patient in spirit is better than the proud in spirit." (Ecclesiastes 7:8 Amplified Bible)

Here's an interesting insight I came across in King Solomon's writings, specifically in the book of Ecclesiastes.

One thing I've learned from enjoying creation and wanting effective results is that it's much better to see the end of an effort than to see its start.

I have experienced the exciting moment of launching a new project and getting the people around me excited about the many possibilities it can create. It is truly an emotional high.

But despite all this, I have also experienced the reality of only going halfway through a project—which, in turn, caused a lot of disappointment and discouragement for me and those around me.

As I reflected on what Solomon said in this particular verse, I asked the Lord why it is better to experience the end from the beginning—if the beginning is so exciting and full of positive emotion and promise!

Here's what the Lord told me: "David, read the second part of this verse. Read with a broken spirit, and you will hear my heart. This is how the second part reads: **"...and the patient in spirit is better than the proud in spirit."**

The Holy Spirit showed me the heart of God through my many efforts. Being patient in spirit is really what the Lord tries to teach anyone aiming to accomplish something in life.

The proud in spirit is someone who constantly makes mistakes because he is very emotional; he listens to his flesh, is usually guided by his flesh, and as a result, is betrayed by his flesh, in this order.

The person who practices patience in spirit is the one who begins with the end in mind. He is willing to pay the price to visualize the future. He is highly spiritual and maintains emotional stability. By emotional stability, I mean that God's emotions govern him first, and then everything flows from that stability. Not the other way around.

The proud often fall into various follies. They lack divine emotional stability.

Here is the key to all success: spiritual and emotional stability that aligns with God's heart.

With everything in you—study and learn this important secret. Neh'enah.

6

Taking Time to Listen!
Why Listening Will Reduce Your Headaches in Life.

During my "Quiet Time"—a personal moment of worship and Bible meditation—I discovered one of the most impactful verses in Proverbs that revealed the "mystery" of why people don't excel, change, reach their full potential, or improve their financial situation. Give me a few minutes of your valuable time, and you'll also have the chance to start living the "good life" based on God's Word.

In Proverbs 1:20-21, these words are spoken: **"Wisdom cries aloud in the street, she raises her voice in the markets; She cries at the head of the noisy intersections** [in the chief gathering places]; **at the entrance of the city gates, she speaks."** What does all this mean? If you're unfamiliar with the Holy Scriptures, let me offer some insight from my perspective.

Before we start, you may wonder, "What is wisdom?" Wisdom is the quality or state of being wise; knowledge of what is true or right combined with sound judgment for action; sagacity, discernment, or insight.

The Scripture above states that wisdom is crying out loudly in the streets, raising her voice in the markets. In this passage, wisdom is personified (as if a real person were calling out). Wisdom is calling or crying out for someone to notice! In short, wisdom is crying out to be heard, and we aren't listening!

Now, pay attention to where wisdom is crying out—it's calling from the streets where people pass by; it's crying out at the markets, where folks are busy buying and trading! Nothing makes it harder to hear wisdom than being too busy to listen.

Take a moment to consider this: Wisdom is shouting loudly so it can be heard, but passersby are not noticing; they are not paying attention. Why? It's obvious that people are too busy with their lives, worries, and future plans to stop and listen to wisdom! Does it seem repetitive? It is!

My dear friends, wisdom isn't just a collection of well-crafted sentences meant to sound poetic! Wisdom is like keys that open doors, and those doors represent the many opportunities you'll encounter in your life.

Too often, we miss a turn in our lives simply because we don't know where to go or what to do. A lack of wisdom leaves us out in the cold and wishing things were different. It's this absence of wisdom that has ruined many lives, marriages, businesses, ministries, churches, careers, and more.

I don't know about you, but time is valuable. We need to keep moving forward and learn as much as we can about life; we must dedicate ourselves to gaining wisdom and applying it in our lives! One man said, "Don't be a follower; be a learner!" I fully agree.

People often think that being busy means they are making progress, but that's not always true! Busyness can hide a trap. If we don't take time to listen to wisdom, we'll keep spinning our wheels until we're exhausted, with nothing to show for it! I believe wisdom can save us from chasing after "shadows."

If we can slow down our "busyness" even just enough to listen to the cry of wisdom and learn what we need to know, I truly believe we will discover a more balanced life, making life more satisfying and fulfilling.

Ignoring wisdom often leads to burnout! Everyone moves in a direction—those who reach their goals are the ones who know where they're going. Don't let the "noise" drown out the voice of wisdom in your life.

You will need wisdom to open future doors! With all thy getting, get wisdom! Have a wonderful day and enjoy this reading. Neh'enah.

7

The Power of Creativity
Why Your Creativity Will Create Your Future!

"Now Bezalel and Oholiab, and every skillful person in whom the LORD has put skill and understanding to know how to perform all the work in the construction of the sanctuary, shall perform in accordance with all that the LORD has commanded." (Exodus 36:1)

A key trait of a good leader is being creative instead of just copying others' ideas.

Much has been given to us by the Creator Himself. Ignoring the creativity that God has abundantly provided would shortchange ourselves and our futures.

I can't think of anything that could take away from an amazing life full of opportunities more than ignoring or dismissing the gift of creativity inside us.

So, what exactly is creativity, or what does it mean to be creative? First, let me say that the root of the word "create" is the foundation of creativity. Merriam-Webster's Dictionary defines "create" as:
1. To make or produce (something): to cause (something new) to exist.
2. To bring (a particular situation) into existence.
3. To produce (something new, like a work of art) by using your talents and imagination.

Based on this definition from Merriam-Webster's Dictionary, we can say that creating is producing something into existence by using our talents and imagination.

Why is creativity such a powerful force within us? I think it's because creativity provides us with the opportunity to craft a better future filled with goodness and blessings—both in ourselves and through us—for the benefit of others.

When creating, the only real limit is our mindset. Whatever you think—can be brought into existence! Once you see it and believe it, it's as good as done. If you think you can, you can. If you think you can't, then you won't.

Let's consider the advantages of being a creative person. First, being creative can free you from the pressure of competition. Some people live to create, while others live to imitate someone else. There's nothing wrong with copying, but why do that when you can use your creativity to shape your own future?

Something powerful happens when you create. There's a deep sense of satisfaction that comes from inventing, creating, or discovering something new. An internal explosion of joy occurs within you! Why the explosion? Because, at your core, you were made to create!

On the other hand, when you compete against others or try to copy someone else's success, you might find yourself crossing lines—cheating, bargaining, pulling strings, playing mind games, stepping over others, and so on—all just to get ahead. Why imitate when you can create?

Remember, when we create using the imagination God has given us, we act according to the pattern inside us. The creations we produce will add value to the world. Over time, people will recognize what we are making—this attraction will bring them to us, helping us succeed in our own creative efforts. All glory to Jesus the King for this!

Additionally, when we create, if our hearts are pure, our projects will be pure as well. Genuine expressions of love, joy, and peace will mirror who and what we are.

I believe it's your time to create. Your creativity will guide you, and you may never have to work another day in your life! Your creativity will lead you to a place of abundance. Remember, if you use what God has given you to create, you will build a future—not just for yourself, but also for others. Neh'enah.

8

What Is Your Philosophy of Failure?

"The steps of a [good] man are directed and established by the Lord when He delights in his way [and He busies Himself with his every step]. Though he falls, he shall not be utterly cast down, for the Lord grasps his hand in support and upholds him." (Psalm 37:23, 24)

Today, I want to discuss a subject that not many people address or dare to talk about. I believe this topic should be discussed more often, studied, and even taught. Let me talk to you about failure.

What is failure? Why do some people get devastated by it? Why do others become stronger because of it?

Merriam-Webster defines failure as "a lack of success or falling short." It's clear that the word carries a negative connotation and implies decline — unless our outlook is different or positive.

Let me emphasize that failure can be the most excellent tool for shaping you, or it can be the "little rock" that trips you up and knocks you out of the race! How we handle failure determines how far and how high we will go! We will either see it as "devastating" or as "educational" – the choice is ours alone.

Failure can have many negative effects and can lead to 1) discouragement, 2) frustration, 3) hesitation, and/or 4) paralysis.

I have lived long enough to witness its negative effects, and it's really no fun – not at all!

Initially, failure hits you, and immediate introspection begins. We start looking inward for reasons things didn't work out or where we failed; then it gets worse—we begin judging ourselves as incompetent and un-qualified for the task. We endure an "emotional brutal beating" and get down on ourselves. Maybe you've never done that, but I have (not going to tell you how many times, though).

Once discouragement sets in, we begin to feel upset with ourselves. We compare our success to others in the same field and wonder why we can't get it right. It doesn't end there.

After feeling upset, we start to think maybe this isn't the right job. "Maybe it's not the right timing, or I should try something else." "Perhaps I should look for something more attainable" — in short, something where I won't fail. Then, we begin to veer away from our calling. I'm sure you've been in this place.

I believe the worst blow happens when we choose not to get up and try again. We feel so "down and out" that we want to give up. Quitting is al-ways an option, but it's not a good one! When feelings of quitting come up, we've entered a paralyzing stage. Beware!

Always remember: You can only "quit" when you're at your peak.

Failure is a tool for purification. It's a fiery furnace that separates men from boys and women from girls. Failure is unavoidable if you're aiming for success. You'll be tested and tried by its fires.

Let's move forward and view failure as a helpful learning experience.

Failure can be what 1) frees you, 2) empowers you, 3) prepares you, and 4) pushes you forward with renewed passion and purpose.

When failure occurs, we must rapidly — and I repeat, rapidly — shift into "educational" mode. This should happen immediately once you realize you've failed.

Some may think you're crazy, others might criticize you, but if you jump into "educational" mode before your critics (including yourself) get to you, you will soon overcome.

Failure can sometimes serve to release you. It can free you to explore new possibilities. Occasionally, the process of elimination works wonders. You might try this and that, and if it doesn't work, try again until you find the right fit! Failure in one area can lead you to another opportunity.

When you finally break free from failure, you enter an empowering stage. You'll feel that you've gained valuable lessons that no one else could have taught you. You'll be adding depth and substance to your personal growth. Amazing!

Adopting an "educational" mindset after failure will motivate you to keep trying and learning. You'll discover different ways of doing things — often "how not to do it." You will become a mentor to many! Soon, you'll be on your way to mastery.

After overcoming the defeatist attitude toward failure, you'll be ready to try again and pursue new ventures and dreams. You will begin creating a remarkable future for yourself and others. Isn't failure a good teacher? Although the lessons can be costly, you will graduate with honors in the school of failure!

What do you gain from your failure curriculum? You gain education, character, experience, and a deeper appreciation for life.

In closing, I challenge you to venture into the deep. So, what if things don't turn out as hoped? Try again! You'll never know unless you do. All I know is, if you make failure one of your learning tools, you will never truly lose! Neh'enah.

9

The Important vs. The Urgent!
Which One Will Stand the Storms of Life?

Today, I want to share with you the different mindsets and philosophies behind why some people find it so difficult to develop character and repeatedly fail to become impactful and influential to others.

I know there are many key factors influencing this, but in my view, nothing hampers maturity more than the idea I'm about to share.

In the book of Matthew 7:24-27, the Scripture reads: **"So everyone who hears these words of Mine and acts upon them [obeying them] will be like a sensible (prudent, practical, wise) man who built his house upon the rock. And the rain fell and the floods came and the winds blew and beat against that house; yet it did not fall, because it had been founded on the rock. And everyone who hears these words of Mine and does not do them will be like a stupid (foolish) man who built his house upon the sand. And the rain fell and the floods came and the winds blew and beat against that house, and it fell—and great and complete was the fall of it."**

As you read these words directly from Jesus, you'll see that Jesus considered the future. The wise man plans ahead; the foolish man focuses on today! Do you understand? It illustrates two people who want to build—one is wise and plans for the future, while the other, foolish (stupid), only concerns himself with today. What makes these two builders different?

In my short life, I have realized that "fast and desperate" builders tend to create flimsy and weak structures—almost as if the energy they put into their work affects everything they do! They often end up doing the work twice or earning a bad reputation as poor builders. It will cost more money to redo the work and can lead to a lot of trouble, not to mention financial stress!

On the other hand, the wise builder carefully considers the cost. He wisely searches for a good location to establish a solid foundation and (without a doubt) knows that the structure will withstand severe weather. The difference, you might ask, is that one felt it was urgent to build the house, while the other believed it was more important to build a strong foundation. Which one would you be?

I recently heard a story about a woman who filed her income tax return and falsely claimed more dependents than she had. She received a large refund and celebrated her victory with thousands of dollars in her bank account. A few years later, she received a letter requesting explanations about her dependents; now she's being audited for lying. What's the result of taking the quick and easy way to make money? You guessed it: paying back the IRS with interest or face the consequences! How smart is that? People often make the same mistake of pursuing what's urgent instead of what's truly important! They prefer to get money now and pay later!

Often, you hear about cases like this one or even worse; yet, people never seem to learn the consequences of chasing what is urgent instead of what is truly important.

Holding ourselves accountable to the principle of always pursuing value will ensure a better future in our efforts. Build for the future; build so others can enjoy; build so others can grow and become; and yes, build eternal foundations for the benefit of others!

Before I end this word, I want to tell you that if you learn to live by a good set of values, your life will be stable, and your foundation will be solid!

If you focus on building a strong foundation of principles and values and don't waver by chasing after the urgent (a feeling we get when we sense pressure to do something other than our set principles or values), your life will attract everything you need to be a true success.

From now on, let's lay solid foundations for God's glory! Neh'enah.

10

The Motivated Learner!

"I went by the field of the lazy man, and by the vineyard of the man void of understanding; And, behold, it was all grown over with thorns, and nettles were covering its face, and its stone wall was broken down. Then I beheld and considered it well; I looked and received instruction. Yet a little sleep, a little slumber, a little folding of the hands to sleep—So shall your poverty come as a robber, and your want as an armed man." (Proverbs 24:30-34 Amplified Version)

Could you develop a habit of learning? Absolutely! Learning is the vehicle that takes you to the realm of greatness. Though it may seem tedious and hardly exciting at first, learning will eventually rise to the surface, becoming a strong foundation for you, your life, and your future.

As a self-motivated learner, your life will always be filled with experiences, opportunities, possibilities, and, of course, a few challenges.

A few years ago, while studying some material for a course I was teaching, I came across an article that referenced a survey about college graduates. The article stated that less than 10% of college graduates ever pick up a book to read after receiving their diplomas (national average).

Wow! How can this be? Many people do only what is expected of them and nothing more! Is it any wonder that many college graduates struggle to find decent jobs? It's not that they aren't smart; it's that they lack interest in learning about life altogether.

Someone asked me recently why I love reading and studying so much. My response was, "I want to create the future for my life and help others do the same!" In case you didn't realize it, every moment you spend studying to improve your life also prepares you to make others' lives more valuable and powerful.

Why not become students of life? Why not take advantage of the wisdom that has been shared with you through books, manuals, tapes, CDs, DVDs, conferences, seminars, and more? Don't waste your time on worthless things; seek out those that will bring and add value to your life. Over time, you will see how these things build an empire of greatness and a life to match!

Self-motivated learners are individuals who research, study, learn new principles, apply them, and then teach others. They recognize the importance of learning; they understand that learning isn't just for themselves — it's never only about them.

What motivates them to study late into the night? Others! What pushes them to spend long hours on research and learning? Others! Why do they spend money on books and CDs? Others! What drives them to sacrifice money and time? You guessed it — OTHERS!

Today, I challenge you to become a self-motivated learner! Don't do it just because I say so. Do it because you see the value in it! Do it because you envision the future — for yourself, your family, your career, your ministry or vocation, and for those yet to come!

May the spirit of a learner come upon you powerfully! Neh'enah.

11

Fruitfulness Begins Here!
4 Key Seeds for a Personal Harvest

"In this, the Father is glorified, that you will bring forth much fruit and that you will be my disciples." (John 15:8 Aramaic Bible)

One of the things I have learned in my life as a "facilitator of instruction" is that if my life is to be effective in touching someone else's, it must be felt first. The old saying goes: If you don't have it, you can't give it! I truly believe this philosophy. Our lives are just conduits; we can only give what is inside of us.

In my devotion today, I want to highlight a few things I believe can help your day flow smoothly and lead to productivity. There's nothing quite like ending your day feeling accomplished and efficient.

Here are some things I do before leaving my house in the morning.

A time for prayer and worship. I strongly believe that all life comes from the Lord God Almighty. I trust that Jesus Christ rules and reigns over my life and that He is the only source that sustains me. He created all things, and without Him, nothing exists today. So, it's clear that if I believe life comes from God's throne, then I will spend time in His presence. Not doing so would be cutting my life short! I need His life within me!

A healthy spiritual life is crucial for any purpose in life. Without it, you are just an empty shell. It's like having a beautiful bottle of expensive perfume made of precious crystal, but with no perfume inside! What value does it have—hardly any at all!

Your spirit-man needs to be nourished, disciplined, aligned with God's heart, and empowered by God's vision. When you prioritize this essential practice, your creative abilities will flourish! Remember Stephen Covey's wise words, "Put first things first!"

It's a good time to journal about your experience with God. I strongly support journaling.

Writing down your thoughts and discoveries after spending time in God's presence is vital for your spiritual health. This journaling moment is a personal time between you and the Lord. It's an important opportunity to record revelation knowledge, creative ideas, and future plans.

Nothing makes you more accountable than putting God's thoughts on paper. I challenge you to buy a nice journal, set aside time after praying, and write, write, write. You'll be glad you did.

Get a good workout early in the morning. Some people dislike waking up early, and maybe they have their reasons. I've found that nothing makes my day feel more productive than rising early to do spiritual and physical exercises. Someone asked me recently if rising early is a natural habit. I said, "No!" I still set my alarm, and I still struggle with sleep, pillows, and blankets!

Why do I do it then? Because I don't want to live with pain. Which pain? The pain of regret! One of my mentors puts it this way: "You will live with one of two pains: the pain of discipline OR the pain of regret!" Pick your pain.

My routine is simple: I work out from Monday through Friday. For my daily workout, I like to run or jog 2 to 3 miles. After I finish my run, I do some floor exercises and stretching. I can't fully explain how working out helps me release worries, anxieties, mental blocks, and stress.

All I know is that a good cardio workout is vital for feeling good! I usually spend about 45 minutes each day on my workout. I'm not a doctor or fitness expert, but if you haven't had a good cardio session in a while, it's smart to talk to a doctor about how much exercise you can safely do—just a suggestion.

Review your daily goals and renew your desire to complete your tasks. Having a list of goals keeps you motivated. Setting clear objectives boosts your efficiency and productivity. Without a plan, your time will "fly by." Before you know it, you might ask, "Where did all my time go?" and realize it's your own fault! Your life can make a difference—if you take time to plan your day and work diligently to accomplish your tasks.

Here are some of my secrets to leading a more fulfilling and effective lifestyle. I understand that people often measure success by their achievements, and that might be true. However, I've realized that real success isn't about material possessions; it's about becoming—becoming a person of value! Neh'enah.

12

Are You In a "Rut?"
Overcoming Apathy, Confusion & Other Dream Killers!

"It is the Lord who goes before you. He will be with you; He will not leave you or forsake you. Do not fear or be dismayed." (Deuteronomy 31:8 ESV)

Have you ever woken up to your alarm, only to hit snooze and sleep for another thirty minutes to an hour? Then, when you finally open your eyes, you stare at the ceiling for a long time, wondering what's next in your life. You start to go into deep introspection about your personal life and realize you haven't done anything meaningful with it! Nothing seems to stir or motivate you, and "isolation" has become your best friend lately. My friend, let me tell you, "You are in a rut!" I'm sure you've experienced this at some point in your life.

Today's devotion aims to share some things that might help you break out of the "rut" you could be in.

Before you can escape a "rut," you need first to understand what a "rut" is and then acknowledge that you're in one.

What is a "rut"? Webster's Dictionary defines it as: a track worn by a wheel or by habitual passage; b: a groove in which something runs. So, it's safe to say that a "rut" is doing the same thing repeatedly until it becomes unattractive and boring.

Sometimes, this feeling hits us hard, and we can't shake it off. We wake up one morning feeling that life is dull and without purpose.

I don't know about you, but I've had my fair share of "ruts." I've reached a point where I don't want to read another word, page, or book; I don't want to talk to another person; I don't want to see another pen or pencil; I don't want to look at my "things to do" list, and frankly, I just want to disappear. I'm sure you've experienced this too.

Today, I want to share how I navigate these "ruts" and how I renew and empower myself to "keep on keeping on" in this incredible journey of life.

If you're in a "rut" today, give yourself permission to experience it. It's okay to be there — really! "Ruts" come and go, so don't think your life is over or your dreams will never come true. It's just a "rut," for crying out loud!

Here are a few things I do when I get stuck:

First, I admit that I am in a "rut." Whenever your energy drops, recognize that you're about to enter one. Rest and sleep help, but they're not enough. The low energy will recover somewhat with rest, but much of the renewal comes from assessing what's important in your life and what's not.

Here's what I do: I take time to realign and reorganize my priorities. I do this by putting everything on hold. (The only way to regain vision and purpose is by shutting down everything around you and taking time to write down what matters most to you.) I return to the place where proper rest can be found — in God's presence. Who else can understand your deepest battles and anxieties better than the Spirit of God?

Once I find peace in God, my joy comes back. When my joy returns, my clarity is restored, and I start feeling renewed.

The final step I take is picking up my "Things to Do" booklet and listing all the things that genuinely matter to me and the purpose for which I was called.

The second thing I consciously address is the voices I listen to. What am I listening to? Who am I listening to?

Sometimes I need to adjust my thoughts, especially if they're negative—self-condemning, degrading, or expressing doubt.

And I make sure to stay away from negative people!

Believe it or not, "ruts" often creep in subtly and can become obstacles for your future. We must align with the purpose for which we were created.

Next time you feel yourself slipping into a "rut," change your scenery. Shake up your situation by trying some of the tips I shared. They've worked for me for nearly 30 years, and I'm still here - I think they work! Neh'enah.

13

The Trap to Progress!

"The Lord our God spoke to us at Horeb, saying, 'You have stayed long enough at this mountain. 'Turn and set your journey, and go to the hill country of the Amorites, and to all their neighbors in the Arabah, in the hill country and in the lowland and in the Negev and by the seacoast, the land of the Canaanites, and Lebanon, as far as the great river, the river Euphrates. 'See, I have placed the land before you; go in and possess the land which the Lord swore to give to your fathers, to Abraham, to Isaac, and to Jacob, to them and their descendants after them." (Deuteronomy 1:6- 8)

Whenever I hear the words "the comfort zone," I never feel that being there is a positive thing. In fact, those words usually have a negative connotation ninety-nine percent of the time.

I personally dislike it when someone tells me, "You are in a comfort zone!" At first, it offends me, then I reflect on it and accept that I might be in a comfortable state and need to push myself to get out of it.

The comfort zone is exactly what it is—a zone of comfort.

What does a comfort zone do for you? Well, for one, it gives a sense of security. It also provides tranquility (peace of mind). The comfort zone has become a place where people find rest from life's tempests and storms. Yes, people run to their comfort zone and stay there until someone challenges it.

Well, you might think that the comfort zone isn't a bad place, and you might even believe it's a good spot to be! Well . . .

Before you consider changing your address to *"Comfort Zone Avenue,"* let me share some of the drawbacks of staying in a comfort zone:

The first thing I notice about living in a comfort zone —being negative —is how it kills your desire for the vision you hold. Too often, people don't reach their desired goals because of setbacks and similar obstacles, so they settle for just getting by. This is not a good thing!

You can make excuses and come up with countless reasons for staying at the halfway point; however, when you close your eyes at night, you'll hear a voice from deep within saying, "You are not at the point you need to be ... climb, climb, climb!"

I believe this is a habit that everyone needs to develop if they want to finish their race. People who see life from God's perspective won't stay in their comfort zone!

Another reason staying in the comfort zone isn't beneficial is that it can freeze or paralyze your creativity. God has given His creation creative power.

As you continuously work to shape your future and others', your creativity is sparked within you. If you explore these opportunities to find answers that define your generation, you will be creative. Staying in a comfort zone only dulls you, and the creative part of you gradually stops.

Finally, living in a comfort zone requires little to no faith at all. If you stay in a comfort zone, your faith doesn't grow the same way it would if you were outside of it.

Living outside the comfort zone ignites your faith. The ability to fully trust God with the outcome of your life is a compelling quality.

Faith in who God is, faith in who you are, and faith in what God has placed in your heart to do with your life are essential keys for anyone who wants to realize their God-given potential.

I challenge you today to step into the unknown; yes, to that place where your fears and doubts have been holding you back. Some things come and fall into your lap effortlessly, but life-changing opportunities are waiting for you to "come and get them!"

Today is the day to start breaking free from that mental prison, your comfort zone! Neh'enah.

14

What Is Your Heart Crying After?

"For we are God's workmanship, created in Christ Jesus to do good works, which God prepared in advance as our way of life." (Ephesians 2:10 – Berean Study Bible)

When discussing purpose, we immediately face the question of what we are meant to do with it. As you know, some people have this very clear in their minds, while others are still searching for the actual reason for their existence.

Life is a gift from God with a purpose. Those who understand this will seek to discover the "why" of their existence.

I've often heard people say, "My life just happened. I'm here now!" My friends, life doesn't just happen—it happens with a greater purpose.

The truth is that God planned everything long before our parents even met. God had a dream or purpose to do something or possess something, and that's where you and I come in - He created us according to His purpose and His desire! You and I were made to bring God pleasure. Powerful stuff! He has a passion, and you and I are called to fulfill it.

When the Lord created the earth, He did so according to His desire. All creation exists for His pleasure and His purpose. Every plant, animal, tree, sun, moon, and star - they only do what they are meant to do — bear fruit, provide shade, shine during the day or night. Each time they express their nature, they are saying, "It is for God's pleasure!' The fish swim, the birds fly, the roses display their beautiful colors — all for His delight.

Now, let's explore humanity: What is our purpose? How do we discover it? How can we tell if we are called to do this or that?

Years ago, a dear friend and mentor gave me a book written by an author (whose name I don't remember) and said, "Read it and understand it; it will change your life!" The title was "Follow Your Heart."

In this book, I learned that inside my inner self (the deepest part of me, often called the heart), there is a cry that seeks fulfillment. Nothing can truly satisfy this inner part except obeying what the heart is pleading for. When you respond to your heart's cry, it feels content and fulfilled. If your heart is crying out for attention, nothing else will satisfy it but its strong desire. Learn to listen for that cry, understand what it is, and then commit yourself to fulfilling it at any cost.

Throughout life, we experience these heartfelt cries. It's God's way of reminding us, "This is my desire burning in you. I have placed my desire in you! Go and fulfill my purpose! If you do, you will always find joy, satisfaction, and contentment, and throughout your life you will reflect my nature to the world."

My point is: You find the "why" of your existence by listening to your heart's most resounding cry. Once you discover the "why," the "how" will come naturally. Neh'enah.

15

It's Like Climbing a Ladder!

During a short vacation, I thought about goal setting. Ideas like under-standing the importance of setting goals, having the stamina to reach them, and experiencing the joy of achieving them are key to progressing in one's calling.

While focusing on my future and what I need to do to get there, thoughts about failure also crossed my mind. I started to wonder why some people are on the path of failure without realizing it—how some only see "the mountain top" but never actually reach it! Immediately, I dismissed the idea of failing in my own life.

During my "get-away," I realized several things about failure. Here are some facts:

1. Failure manifests in our lives in very subtle ways.
2. Failure is always near and ready to take what you give it.
3. Failure is always waiting for an opportunity to emerge if it is taken for granted.
4. Failure refuses to apologize for destroying your dreams.
5. Failure is responsible for destroying countless plans, dreams, and visions.

While reflecting on how my life has experienced failure, I quickly realized what NOT to do to avoid failure or stay on the path to success. Here are some of the truths I've discovered and continue to apply as I write these few lines.

If you want to stay on track to reach your dreams, plans, and goals, my advice to you is the following:

Have a vision for your life. Without vision, people perish, as the Holy Scriptures teach. If you can't see your future, you'll find it hard to accomplish almost anything in life. You may become everyone's servant; you'll be working for someone else's goals; and your life may never reach its full potential.

A vision is the ability to see what is invisible! What does the vision of your heart envision? What do you see yourself doing with your life? A hammer is used to drive nails, a saw is used to cut wood, and a baker bakes bread—what about you? If you don't have a vision for your life, seriously take time to meditate on this.

Secondly, set goals to achieve that vision. If you want to start a business, what kind of business should it be? I recommend choosing one that you are passionate about. Passion and perseverance are essential when things get tough or obstacles arise. With these qualities, you will be able to overcome every challenge without doubt.

Remember, as a rule, that a business is all about serving. The motive should be pure and focused on giving—not taking! It's about using your company, gift, or vision to solve someone's problem or meet a need. If you prioritize others first, you will be rewarded later. I love this philosophy.

Always create a list of goals that will help you reach your desired vision. Write down your goals, regardless of how many they are. Then begin working your way toward success.

Thirdly, continue working steadily on those goals with clear focus. Many people fail to reach their dreams and goals because they are too anxious, overly self-absorbed in ego, impatient, and too distracted by the results. People forget to focus only on the next step in their goal list, which truly matters.

Remember, when you climb a ladder, you usually don't skip steps; otherwise, you might fall and hurt yourself. Children often try to do illogical things like that, but hopefully not you. You should have enough sense. Your focus should always be on step two of your goals!

I believe that the main reason we don't reach our goals is not primarily fear and doubt, but rather a lack of vision and clear goal setting. We tend to overlook discipline!

And finally, avoid distractions. Distractions can take many forms. It could be someone who doesn't believe in you and only says negative things; it might be that you have fallen into the "get successful or rich quickly" mindset, or you could be distracted by people who waste your valuable time.

Remove anything that distracts you from what truly matters and your goals right away! It will only divert your focus and make you wonder why your life isn't progressing.

Before I conclude this blog, it would be wise and beneficial to take some time to reflect on where you currently stand. What is your vision? Does it still inspire passion within you? Have you set goals to achieve them? Or have you been distracted by trivial things? Today is the perfect day to get everything in order and pursue it! Neh'enah.

16

Keep the Fire Burning!

"Then I said to them, "You see the distress that we are in, how Jerusalem lies waste, and its gates are burned with fire. Come and let us build the wall of Jerusalem, that we may no longer be a reproach." And I told them of the hand of my God which had been good upon me, and also of the king's words that he had spoken to me. So they said, "Let us rise up and build." Then they set their hands to this good work." (Nehemiah 2:17-18)

Have you ever noticed that many God-given ideas come your way, but these ideas rarely develop into something meaningful? God is constantly sharing His heart with us, and it's our responsibility to bring those ideas to life.

I have heard many people talk about their vision and list their ideas and goals, but for one reason or another, those ideas vanish into the wind!

I have come to believe that life should be lived "on the attack." We should all strive to accomplish things instead of waiting for something to happen. I have learned and wholeheartedly believe that a law exists that kills, destroys, or decays – it is called the Law of Negligence. If you neglect something, it will die, decay, or corrode.

The word negligence comes from the word negligent. What does negligent mean? Merriam-Webster's dictionary defines it as failing to take proper or routine care of something or someone.

Neglecting to take care of something and leaving it unattended is considered negligence.

Now, when it comes to ideas, dreams, or visions, the law of negligence also applies. Its goal is to prevent what could happen from happening. One of our biggest enemies is negligence! *The rule is that if you keep paddling forward, you will eventually get somewhere. If you don't paddle, you will stay in the same place.*

How can we overcome the law of negligence when it comes to the ideas and visions we receive to create meaningful change in our lives, ministry, or careers? Once you have a vision or idea to achieve something great, you want to keep it fresh by:

1. Take the time to write down your vision and/or idea, and date it! Once you have something worth pursuing or acting on, write it down and include as many details as possible. This will serve as the foundation for your vision and/or idea. It will serve as your motivation when times get tough, and your energy runs low. After writing it down, date it. This will remind you when you received the idea and help you build on it with deadlines for achievements, etc.

2. Consistently read materials related to your subject. Whatever your vision or idea may be, look for resources and reading materials you can explore. Nothing builds momentum like a good book on the topic you want to bring to life. Make time to read daily. This will help progress your vision. Remember, transformation starts in the mind first, then in action!

3. Consistently listen to materials on the subject. If you don't have a CD player in your car, buy one. Turn your vehicle into a mobile learning station. You can listen to music at another time – give yourself the chance to learn life-changing principles during your commute. Music might improve your mood, but principles will help you become a valuable person.

4. Sharing your ideas and vision with those who share your heart is essential. There are many people around us daily: family, friends, acquaintances, teachers, and mentors. While they all play a role in our lives, only a few truly influence us. Who are the people speaking into your life? Who pushes you out of the "comfort zone" or "box"? Who encourages you to dream bigger? Do you have their names on a list? How many are there—just one, two, or three? Probably not a very long list, right? Remember, mentors are teachers who enter our lives to help us grow to the next level. Share your heart with them, and they can propel you forward.

5. Avoid sharing your vision and ideas with negative people. Negativity will always be around us. These are the folks who can't see you growing, creating, achieving new heights, or dreaming bigger. Do you have any of those? Of course – we all do! Usually, our list of "naysayers" is longer than our list of mentors. Now, we have a choice: we can listen to negative thoughts or surround ourselves with positive people. That decision is ours! Remember, we become what we listen to. I'm sure you can figure it out.

6. Going back to your vision statement and regularly reading your purpose when you're feeling discouraged, lost, or confused can be very helpful. We all face standstills, setbacks, potholes in the road, heartbreaks, discouragement, and even confusion at times. Have you been there? We all go through these moments, but they are no reason to stop pursuing our dreams and ideas. I often write down my thoughts and date them. When I hit a pothole, I take out my journal and revisit the core of my vision. Doing this quickly restores my drive, passion, and fire. Many people have buried their visions and ideas — and I believe it was often by choice. They could have kept them alive, but they failed to write them down and date them. Accountability for our dreams is essential!

Every vision and idea needs to be followed up on. They must be cultivated and watered daily. Failing to attend to them might cause them to dissipate and vanish completely. Let me reiterate that keeping a journal of all your visions and ideas wouldn't be a bad idea. Write them down and date them. Believe it or not, they will be your greatest treasures. Neh'enah.

17

Manifesting the Hidden Treasures of the Heart!

"So do not throw away your confidence; it will be richly rewarded. You need to persevere so that when you have done the will of God, you will receive what he has promised." (Hebrews 10:35-36)

The past few weeks have been full of assessment and accomplishments. We're already in mid-October, and the end of the year is approaching.

How much of your yearly goals have you been able to achieve? How many of those goals are still "miles away" from being reached? Do you understand what I mean? Has this ever happened to you? One thing I know: it is not the most exciting feeling in the world! In fact, this very real emotion, if not kept in check, can lead to depression or discouragement! Do you know what I mean?

At the beginning of each year, I dedicate my heart and mind to reaching several goals and projects. These range from personal milestones to professional or ministerial successes. I'm not sure exactly when or where I learned to do this, but setting goals for the new year has always kept me motivated, focused on what matters, and eager for greater accomplishments.

As I reviewed my list, I started evaluating each project. The ones I completed gave me great satisfaction. My sense of fulfillment isn't measured by numbers, money, or popularity; it's defined by how many things hidden in my heart are brought into the open.

The things or projects I didn't complete teach me a few facts: 1) they show me the need for more discipline in my life; 2) they also reveal how easily I can lose focus, meaning I pursue the urgent instead of the important; 3) they teach me that the "bigger picture" can very easily be diminished (in my own mind) due to external pressures or internal fears and inadequacies.

How does someone come to terms with yesterday's lack of accomplishments and tomorrow's life-changing vision?

Here are some key points I've considered regarding what I didn't do and upcoming or future concerns.

1. I see projects and goals as teachers. I don't set goals to see what I can achieve. I've learned to set goals based on how they will change me as I work to accomplish them. When your philosophy is not about what you get, but about what you will become, then you are on your way to a great life.

2. When you face failure and unachieved goals, always look inward. That's the best advice I can give you. Don't focus on those difficult situations; people who were against you, robbed you, or cheated you out of an opportunity, or even circumstances beyond your control. Don't blame anyone; it's no one's fault! If you're ever tempted to make excuses—like being bitter at life because, when you were five, someone stole your lollipop or ice-cream bar—it wasn't anyone's fault but yours for not holding on to that lollipop tighter!

3. If your goals weren't achieved and a new year is coming, don't stress; just add them to your "New Goals List" for the upcoming year. Guess what? You'll need to work a little harder next year to reach them and the new ones as well. If you follow through, you'll become a better person!

What about the new goals and projects? My advice is to keep dreaming, even if you haven't finished your list of goals. Never stop imagining the future! Continue pursuing your heart's desires. Neh'enah.

18

Being Lazy Is Not an Excuse - It's the Result of a Passionless Life!

"But [like a boxer] I strictly discipline my body and make it my slave, so that, after I have preached [the gospel] to others, I myself will not somehow be disqualified [as unfit for service]." (1 Corinthians 9:27 *Amplifed Version*)

I have heard people say that making significant changes in their lives is a very expensive undertaking. "It requires discipline and sacrifice; it is too much, and I don't know if I can pay that cost!" I'm sure you have heard many others with the same mindset.

As the Spirit of the Lord moves within us, we become excited about the "possibilities" of a new season. I used to think this way for years, until I realized that new seasons would bring me whatever I wanted them to. *New seasons in God don't determine my outcome—I determine my outcome through my obedience!*

During times of change and seasons, many prepare themselves with renewed determination. Those pursuing transformation go a step further by buying new running shoes, workout outfits, books, journals, renewing gym memberships, and purchasing new recipes and blenders to make their favorite smoothies, etc. I support this, but there's more to it!

A few years ago, I ran into a friend I hadn't seen since high school. It's been a long time. He told me he was very disappointed in himself. He mentioned that he hadn't had much success in life and was a bit overweight; he didn't know how to change his future.

He also mentioned that he had tried exercise programs, videos, and machines. "As you can see," he went on to say, "I have not lost any weight but am actually bigger than ever; not to mention that all my exercise machines are being used to hang clothes!" Does this sound like something you have seen or heard?

Transformation and change are deeply linked to our mind, heart, and discipline.

To successfully implement any kind of change, there are a few key steps to follow.

First, a person needs to prepare their mind. How do you do this? In my experience, I prepare my mind by filling it with knowledge about what I want to accomplish. For example, if my goal is financial success, I will educate myself on that topic. If my goal is to deepen my spiritual life, I focus on learning more about it. The same principle applies to health, wealth, business, ministry, and so on.

Knowledge is essential for change. The more knowledge you have, the more your actions will reflect what you've read and studied.

Secondly, the person seeking change must also prepare with their heart. What does this mean? Preparing with the heart affects us emotionally; it sparks passion within us. If you lack passion for what you are studying or learning, you won't keep doing it for long. Passion is the driving force behind long-term goals and visions. Many goals fail because of a lack of passion.

Some people do things because they need to, so they discipline themselves to do them; yet others might lack discipline, but their passion keeps pushing them forward. Passion is a burning fire, and it must be fueled daily.

How do you ignite passion? Here's what has worked for me over the years, as I share the third step and element for change.

You fuel passion through simple acts of discipline. I see discipline as logs being added to a barbecue pit. The more logs you add, the bigger the fire. The number of logs you put on the pit determines how strongly the fire burns. If you're too lazy to add logs, then you won't have a fire! It's that simple! Being lazy isn't an excuse - it's a sign of lacking passion.

If you discipline your life by paying attention to the small details, you will never lack passion. Passion will carry you through any change you need to make, whether it's this week, next week, or next year! Neh'enah.

19

Walking in True Harmony with God!
The Recipe for Peace, Joy, and Victory on Earth

Then Jesus said to them, "When you lift up the Son of Man, then you will know that I am He, and that I do nothing of Myself; but as My Father taught Me, I speak these things. And He who sent Me is with Me. The Father has not left Me alone, for I always do those things that please Him." (John 8:28,29)

As I spent some quality time in His presence this morning, the Lord made something very clear to me. He spoke to me about harmony and what it means to be in sync with His Spirit.

The first thing that came to my mind was tuning a guitar. When the guitar is tuned correctly and the chords are played properly, the combination of notes will sound pleasing to the ear and sometimes even produce a sweet tone.

Now, the opposite of this would be an untuned guitar. The sound will be off, making it unpleasant and hard to hear.

Most, if not all, of our lack of peace in life is caused by not walking in harmony with the sound of the Lord flowing in and through us. We expose ourselves to any sound, whether it harmonizes with God or not, and we reap its benefits.

I am continually learning about man's behavior both inside and outside of God's will. What an art this is!

When people walk in harmony with God, their lives are full of peace and joy. When individuals stray from the order set by the Lord, their lives become filled with turmoil and ongoing tests and trials.

People overlook some of these things in their lives. Most are unaware of this kind of living. They look at the church and go there thinking, "They will pray for me, and everything will be better," only to find that nothing has really changed!

The lesson on harmony with God I share with you is a simple way to find peace, victory, and joy in your life.

Note the life of Jesus. Jesus walked with the Father and did everything according to the Father's wishes. John 8:28 and 29 bear this out. Jesus used the word "always." The word "always" in Greek means "at all times."

Because of our imperfections and fleshly tendencies, we might not always be able to keep up with doing this.

What I believe this means is that we are called to always stay in God's will; we must have the consciousness that says, "I am in God's will, and that is what I strive to accomplish every single day!" To be so in tune with this truth that when we veer off even a little from the path of the Father, something inside us cries loudly and groans, saying, "You are out of harmony! Get tuned now!" We quickly run and get back in line.

Being in tune with God and flowing in harmony with Him is truly the path to peace, joy, and victory! Neh'enah.

20

Don't Buy Into Your Emotions Too Quickly!

My hope is built on nothing less
Than Jesus' blood and righteousness;
I dare not trust the sweetest frame,
But wholly lean on Jesus' name.
On Christ, the solid Rock, I stand;
All other ground is sinking sand,
All other ground is sinking sand.

-Edward Mote

One thing I notice often is how people tend to fluctuate emotionally.

It's interesting how any day a person can be upbeat, have a spring in their step, speak words of encouragement, and feel confident that their future is bright and promising.

The next day, all the emotions have shifted. Everything is heading south; nothing that was previously planned turns out as planned. People turn against you, the police stop you for speeding, your friends turn on you, and your checks bounce, racking up huge fees for insufficient funds on every purchase. Ouch!

These kinds of circumstances often cause someone to shift emotionally away from their goals. In such a situation, I say, "Be very careful! Don't buy into it!"

One of the main reasons we set goals and practice discipline is for this very purpose—staying the course despite opposition. Our eyes notice the lack of progress, our mind interprets what we see, and a quick decision is made in our mind and spirit. We either remain committed to the path we initially chose or follow our ever-wavering emotions!

I've spoken to many people about vision, purpose, and similar topics. The stories are mostly the same. A path has been laid out, but a lack of emotional intelligence and discipline has held back many people's potential.

After facing many challenges, someone might say, "I feel God is changing my course!" I, personally, don't believe that a person's course changes just because of obstacles. I know God does change directions and guides us to a new level of growth, but this only happens when the individual has "graduated" from the previous course he was given.

Charting a course must be done intentionally.

If you believe the Lord is guiding you in a specific direction, prepare for it. Map out your plan and set a deadline. If nothing happens by then, let it go! Whose fault is it? Not God's! So, who is to blame? You guessed it – YOURS!

Don't fall for false emotions, obstacles, circumstances, or people's negative words. Don't allow anything external to influence you.

My advice is simple: stay put! Seek God! Before you take any action, ask yourself, "Did I finish the last course? Did I complete the last assignment given by the Spirit of God? Did I accomplish everything that God assigned to me last time?" You must be honest with yourself for progress to happen.

I trust you will heed my words and allow God to reveal a new and living way to stay the course in expanding God's glory here on earth. Neh'enah.

21

Open Up the Door! - Part 1

"Behold, I stand at the door and knock. If anyone hears My voice and opens the door, I will come in to him and dine with him, and he with Me." (Revelation 3:20)

During prayer this week, the Holy Spirit prompted my heart to revisit these verses written above. It is and has been so clear to me that whenever God is preparing to do something in a man or woman of God, He prompts them to pray.

This kind of prayer is not your average kind. It goes beyond the usual and calls for deeper brokenness and obedience. A few years ago, I came across a survey about believers' prayer lives.

The survey indicated that the "so-called" Christian prayed about five minutes a day on average, while the pastor or minister prayed fifteen minutes daily. When I read that survey, the first thing that came to my mind was how we will face the consequences of our prayerlessness in the service of the Christian life and in the world we live in.

It has been years since I read this survey, and the effects of our prayerlessness have become clear a thousand times over! Much of what we see in our world today is due to the prayerlessness of God's people. We like to blame our society, our government, our culture, and even our religion for what happens in our world today; yet deep down, I know the real reason is: it is called prayerlessness! I understand that this is why we are facing a decline in our days—pure prayerlessness!

Dine with Jesus!

Let me lead you into this sacred space I call prayer.

Prayer is recognizing God's knock on our hearts. It's hearing His footsteps approaching the door of our hearts and us moving toward the door to open it for Him! This, in my humble opinion, marks the beginning of a prayer time.

People gather for corporate prayer meetings where most attendees are not seeking God's prophetic knock and voice but are instead waiting to pray for their own personal needs. They form circles, and the complaining begins! I challenge anyone who desires to "dine with Jesus" to keep reading these notes.

Notice the intimate prayer time here. He stands at the door and knocks. It says, **"If anyone hears My voice and opens the door, I will come in to him and dine with him, and he with Me."** If anyone at anytime, anywhere, hears and opens the door, then Jesus will come in and dine with him, and he will dine with Him! Wow!

What Happens While You Dine with Jesus?

Before I reveal this truth, let's understand what the word dine actually means. The original Greek definition of dine means "meal," "chief meal," or "feast." Essentially, Jesus was saying, "If you open the door and let me in, you and I will have a feast! In this feast, I will reveal myself to you and teach you everything you need to know for this season in your life, vocation, ministry, etc."

Here is what you need to understand: Our lives unfold in seasons, inspired by God. So, for each season, it's essential to recognize what God is doing in our lives. As we sit at the table with Jesus, He will teach us the following:
- Our Attitude Toward the Season We Are In. When we acknowledge that God is guiding us through a specific season, it changes how we

feel about life. Often, God's people become confused and start rebuking demons and devils before even understanding who really holds the cup of their pain! [see John 18:11.] As we sit with Jesus, we find emotional balance, and our attitude begins to align with His will.

- Wisdom from God's Perspective on Action. When we sit to hear God's heart, the first thing we gain is wisdom. An impartation of holy perspective and spiritual discernment of "why and when" will come to us immediately. Wisdom is "wise skill." As the Lord spends time with us and we spend time with Him, we will gain many wise skills to follow the blueprint He has designed.

- Leadership Enablement and Ability. It is an incredible thing to receive revelation during times when God visits us, but it's entirely another to know what to do with what we've received. This requires leadership skills at a much higher level than what we're used to. Part of the reason there is so much dissatisfaction among believers today is that they are not acting on what God has shown them; honestly, it's simply because they don't know how! I hear Christian leaders today talk about how much God has revealed to them, yet, at the end of the day, they do nothing about it. Dinner with Jesus will solve this problem.

As I finish this first part, I want to challenge your heart. Along with all you already know, add this one more thing: Learn to become more sensitive to His voice, His knock, and His invitation. Recognition is a valuable key to your future progress. If we listen and obey, we will have food to eat that no one else knows anything of! Neh'enah.

22

Open Up the Door! - Part 2

"He who has my commandments and obeys them--he it is who loves me. And he who loves me will be loved by my Father, and I will love him and will clearly reveal myself to him." (John 14:21 - Weymouth New Testament)

Today, I want to continue sharing my thoughts on God revealing Himself to us. My previous notes highlighted that if we listen and open the door to Him, we will experience a powerful time of revelation as Jesus dines with us and reveals His secrets.

Here's another insight into how God approaches us and reveals Himself to us. Focus on the condition of the heart. It really all boils down to the heart!

- He who has my commandments. As we deepen our relationship with the Lord, making it more personal and intense, we will start to understand what it truly means to internalize God's command ments. If we don't meditate on what God instructs us to do, we will never genuinely take it to heart. Unless commandments become part of us, we will never consistently live by them.

- He who obeys my commandments. The second part of this is obedience itself. When we humble ourselves in His presence during prayer, we will not only personalize His commandments but also take the initiative to "walk them out." If there is one thing God knows about us, it is the intent of our hearts. He knows us better than we know ourselves. Our attitude in prayer, our reception of His commands, and our desire to walk them out will set us on a course that pleases the Lord. Is it any wonder why the Lord manifests Himself to those who are willing to hear and obey God?

- What defines true love for God? What must be visible to prove it? True love is always characterized by one key trait—sacrifice. Without sacrifice, we cannot truly experience this love for God that many speak about. People often say they love God, but their actions don't reflect it. Their actions are missing! Prayer requires a lot of sacrifice. If people aren't willing to give up time to be alone with God, then true love isn't there. Everything about God involves sacrifice.

- Fatherly Attraction: Genuine love for God draws the Father's affection. When our hearts overflow with love for God, it prompts the Father to come closer. If there is one thing God can relate to, it is love. When our hearts are filled with love, God will be drawn to us.

- Jesus will love us in return and clearly reveal Himself to us. As I conclude these notes, it is clear to me that God will visit us when our hearts are filled with love for Him. When our hearts reach a certain depth, God will manifest Himself powerfully and show us His heart. There is a reason why God reveals Himself to us – it is because our hearts are full of love for Him! Neh'enah.

23

Revival in a Cave! – Part 1

"And there he went into a cave, and spent the night in that place; and behold, the word of the Lord came to him, and He said to him, "What are you doing here, Elijah?" (1 Kings 19:9)

Today, I want to share one of the most powerful stories in the Bible about human weakness and God's strength coming together to create a powerful testimony for God's glory!

The story begins with one of God's servants named Elijah. Elijah was a prophet of the Lord and moved with great faith. He prayed often and prayed earnestly before the Lord. He spent much time in prayer and came to understand God's purpose for his life. There is no doubt that this man had a powerful touch of God on his life.

There came a time in Elijah's life when the Lord inspired him to be dedicated and pure; to be a man of holiness and a powerful witness of God's heart to His people. During this period, Elijah observed the wickedness and compromise among God's people. They were worshiping false gods and idols, and Elijah's heart was troubled and even angered by how God's people were living.

So, Ahab sent for all the children of Israel and gathered the prophets together on Mount Carmel. And Elijah came to all the people, and said, **"How long will you falter between two opinions? If the Lord is God, follow Him; but if Baal, follow him."** (1 Kings 18:20-21)

It was here that Elijah challenged all of God's people to choose whom they would serve, Jehovah God or Baal. In this challenge, Elijah confronted and killed 450 prophets of Baal. **And Elijah said to them, "Seize the prophets of Baal! Do not let one of them escape!" So they seized them, and Elijah brought them down to the Brook Kishon and executed them there." (1 Kings 18:40)**

"And Ahab told Jezebel all that Elijah had done, also how he had executed all the prophets with the sword. Then Jezebel sent a messenger to Elijah, saying, "So let the gods do to me, and more also, if I do not make your life as the life of one of them by tomorrow about this time." And when he saw that, he arose and ran for his life, and went to Beersheba, which belongs to Judah, and left his servant there. But he himself went a day's journey into the wilderness and came and sat down under a broom tree. And he prayed that he might die, and said, "It is enough! Now, Lord, take my life, for I am no better than my fathers!" (1 Kings 19:1–4)

When Jezebel heard the news from her feeble husband Ahab, she became furious and vowed to kill Elijah for destroying the false prophets of Baal.

How was Elijah supposed to respond to this? Apparently, there were some repercussions in the heavens. I believe that as one begins to advance in God's kingdom, repercussions do come. One must be ready and prepared to face the challenges.

Elijah's Response

"And when he saw that, he arose and ran for his life, and went to Beersheba, which belongs to Judah, and left his servant there. But he himself went a day's journey into the wilderness and came and sat down under a broom tree. And he prayed that he might die, and said, "It is enough! Now, Lord, take my life, for I am no better than my fathers!"

I'm not sure why, but when Elijah heard Jezebel's threat to kill him, he was overwhelmed with fear. So much so that he practically ran for his life and hid.

Most of us, when faced with a tough situation, tend to react in a similar way—not physically, but spiritually. We often shut down and isolate ourselves from others, feeling very discouraged. Is this some pattern for people who are powerful with words and actions? I believe so.

The Sin of Untimely Relaxation

Here is what I believe is one of the main causes of spiritual warfare – relaxation. Once we have achieved a victory, we tend to become complacent. We rest spiritually, and the enemy gathers himself and launches an assault like a flood.

It's during this relaxation mode that the enemy lulls us to sleep and takes advantage of our slumber. We wake up suddenly, realizing that the enemy is upon us and ready to destroy us. We feel like the enemy has advanced significantly during our sleep, and now we can't collect ourselves to fight.

That is why anyone who desires to live godly in Christ Jesus and follow His call must always remember that they are living in a battle zone twenty-four-seven, three hundred sixty-five days a year.

We become overwhelmed by life's challenges, which leads us to take a detour. Instead of seeking God's best, we settle for mediocrity. Many have gone through this and fallen along the way.

When a victory is achieved, one must stay alert against all opposition from both within and outside! Stay tuned for the second part of this message. Neh'enah.

24

Revival in a Cave! – Part 2

This week, I want to continue with the second part of Revival in a Cave.

The last time I shared with you was about the life of Elijah and how he fled from the wicked Jezebel. I also talked about how relaxing after a great victory can be harmful to our progress in God.

Let me take you deeper this week as we explore Elijah's lonely experience and his cave.

"And there he went into a cave, and spent the night in that place; and behold, the word of the Lord came to him, and He said to him, "What are you doing here, Elijah?" (1 Kings 19:9)

Let me ask the one question the Lord asked Elijah, **"What are you doing here, Elijah?"**

There are times in our walk and service to the Lord when we feel overwhelmed by external things. By external things, I mean outside pressures that come to "blow us away!" But blow us away from where or what? To blow us away from our position in Christ, of course! What else could be more precious to the believer than their position in Christ?

Position in God is Everything!

Look at this now: Elijah is brave and courageous for the Lord His God; he is willing to stand up for Jehovah without hesitation. He is not afraid to face the 450 prophets of Baal or anyone else who might come, for that matter. I don't believe there was a single soul more zealous than Elijah in his day!

However, during a time of victory and celebration, Jezebel sent word to him, promising she would kill Elijah. Elijah ran for his life and hid!

Friends, Jezebel's words caused Elijah to lose confidence in God. The influence of this wicked woman was strong enough to shake a man's faith. Was it that Jezebel's words were extremely powerful, or was it Elijah's choice to doubt Jehovah's power? I believe the latter is true.

It's very possible for a man of God to lose his zeal, strength, and even his confidence in God due to outside forces. Very possible!

The key to overcoming this lies in God's mercy. Once God's servant realizes he's fleeing from the enemy, all he needs to do is stop running and start listening to God's voice. Elijah ran into a cave, and God came to find him there and asked, "What are you doing here, Elijah?"

When in distress, we must decide: Do we listen to the enemy or to God's Spirit? Our results will depend on that choice.

Peter's Invitation

"And Peter answered Him and said, "Lord, if it is You, command me to come to You on the water. So He said, "Come." And when Peter had come down out of the boat, he walked on the water to go to Jesus. But when he saw that the wind was boisterous, he was afraid; and beginning to sink he cried out, saying, "Lord, save me!" (Matthew 14:28-30)

Peter was a man of faith and believed in Jesus. When Jesus invited Peter to "come" to him and walk on water, Peter obeyed and walked in God's way, not his own. This is something to notice. If we walk on His grounds, we have nothing to fear!

The fear "kicked in" when Peter took his eyes off the position Jesus had invited him to. Please understand me, my friends, this has nothing to do with the winds and the waves. The fact is apparent: Peter took his eyes off the position Jesus had placed him in and shifted to "Peter's position" as he started focusing on the winds and the waves. This was the recipe that brought Peter underwater. It will be the same thing that will get you and me underwater!

 Elijah went underwater! It wasn't until the Lord came looking for him and renewed his weary soul that he was set on fire once again!

Remember, it was God who sought out His man, not the other way around. God will always show His mercy if we humble ourselves and trust in Jesus alone. Revival in a cave is possible if we admit our weakness before God and stay remorseful in spirit. Neh'enah.

25

Vision of the Burning Lamp

"Let your waist be girded and your lamps burning; and you yourselves be like men who wait for their master, when he will return from the wedding, that when he comes and knocks they may open to him immediately." (Luke 12:35-36)

"Only one life, twill soon be past,
Only what's done for Christ shall last.
And when I am dying, how happy I'll be,
If the lamp of my life has been burned out for thee."

-CT. Studd

As I reflect on the Scripture our Lord and King Jesus spoke to us, I can't help but think about the great responsibility each servant of the Lord has. The call to walk with and serve Jesus, ignited by holy fire, is not just a nice thought or saying, but a necessity!

Without fire, all we have is a fancy-looking lamp, but it fails to serve its original purpose.

Lamps are useful for providing light and warmth. Without fire, a lamp is just a pretty decoration. In our understanding of God, we must include the need for a life filled with fire! Because without it, to put it mildly, we are truly useless and unproductive for His purposes!

Vision of a Burning Lamp

I just celebrated my 52nd birthday this past week and had a wonderful time with family and friends. One of the highlights was the morning prayer I spent in the Lord's presence that very day.

As I spent time with Jesus in the secret place, thanking Him for my lot in life and the 52 years of precious life He had granted me, I asked the Lord a question: "What does a fifty-two-year-old man look like to you?" Don't ask me why I was asking that, but God knew why, I'm sure. As I waited for the Lord's reply, this is what He showed me:

He showed me a vision of a lamp. *The lamp looked somewhat old and rustic, like those charming antique lamps people buy and display as décor. I heard a voice say to me, "I know that you are trying to guess how old that lamp is." I replied, "Very true." The Lord then showed me the lamp and asked, "Does it really matter how old a lamp is? Is the lamp really all that important?" As I sat pondering the Lord's reply, I saw a hand emerge and lift the lamp. The lamp then began to burn with such brightness because the fire in it was bright and intense! After the lamp burned brightly for a while, the Lord said to me, "David, how old do you think the fire is?" "I don't know. You just turned it on, so I guess it's a few minutes old?" I answered. The Lord then said, "David, my fire is an eternal flame. It is always burning. It is always fresh. It is always new. My plan isn't about the lamp but about the fire! You can feel as fresh and new as you allow Me to burn within you!"* End of vision.

So, for my birthday, besides the special gifts I received, the Lord also gave me a gift—a vision of a burning lamp. This vision has set me on a new path of responsibility. Here's my new prayer, along with King David's: "**O God, You have taught me from my youth, and hitherto I have declared Your wondrous works. Yes, even when I am old and gray-headed, O God, forsake me not,** [but keep me alive] **until I have declared Your mighty strength to** [this] **generation, and Your might and power to all that are to come.**" (Psalm 71:17-18) Neh'enah.

26

Why God Chooses to Test You That Way!

"For as the rain and the snow come down from heaven, and do not return there without watering the earth and making it beat and sprout, and furnishing seed to the sower and bread to the eater; so will My word be which goes forth from My mouth; It will not return to Me empty, Without accomplishing what I desire, And without succeeding in the matter for which I sent it." (Isaiah 55:10, 11)

When tested by the Lord, it is never without purpose. God works deeply within us by using various tools to accomplish His intended result. Christ is being formed in us increasingly as we let His Holy Spirit do this powerful work of grace. The test can last as long as God needs it, for the benefit of shaping us into His image!

The Holy Spirit's Discipline

No one understands the mind of God like the Holy Spirit. In fact, the mind of God is the Spirit of God. It is the Spirit living within us that constantly guides our lives toward certain places, people, and circumstances that present the most significant challenges.

One thing every servant of Jesus must truly understand is this: the Holy Spirit will always lead you to situations that test your character and stretch your faith for greater fruitfulness.

During your pain, complaints, or distress, you may be unaware of what is happening around you – but rest assured that God has your entire life in the palm of His hand! Listen to the promise: "I have engraved you on the palms of my hands. Your walls are always in my presence." (Isaiah

49:16)

If God is testing your life, it's a clear sign that He deeply desires to bring you to a place where He is pleased with you. Never misunderstand the purpose behind God's tests in your life.

He Knows All Things!

God knows exactly what torments us; He sees the very thing that has a stronghold on our lives; He recognizes the things that hinder our progress. Through His loving mercy and grace, He guides us on the path — the way out of the misery we're stuck in!

The pain you and I feel when God is working in us is simply the process of being 'torn away" from a life of sin, compromise, and waywardness. God desires to remove anything that has become an idol in our lives. This process can be excruciating.

The next time you face adversity in your life, before blaming others, before going through endless counseling, and before casting demons out of your life, ask yourself this honest question: Is there rebellion in my life?

If there is rebellion, then you know exactly who is testing you! Neh'enah.

27

"Get Out of the Way!"

"And it came to pass, when the priests came out of the holy place, that the cloud filled the house of the Lord, so that the priests could not continue ministering because of the cloud; for the glory of the Lord filled the house of the Lord." (1 Kings 8:10, 11)

Wow! Have you ever read these verses? What a testimony! God's glory was revealed, and the priests could no longer continue their service in the temple. It says that, "the glory of the Lord filled the house of the Lord."

What do you think caused this, and why? Were the priests offering sacrifices and going about their daily routines at the temple when suddenly a cloud appeared while they prayed and served? It seems that way.

The Principle of Waiting Upon His Glory and His Power

Here's what I believe the Lord wants to teach us in these verses: it's a simple yet powerful lesson.

As we go through our lives and daily routines, we tend to go through the motions, living almost unconsciously. Isn't this true? We rarely make significant changes to our lives, careers, business, or ministry unless we face an obstacle, a crisis, or a New Year's resolution. This is how most people live out their daily lives.

Now, if you want to see some change happen, if you want to add excitement to your lifestyle, invite the glory of God into your situation. As you make your request known to the Lord, buckle up and get ready for the ride of your life!

When we call on Him and wait with a desperate heart, the Lord Himself will come and fill us with His glory.

When His Glory Comes, Then What?

When His glory finally appears and His Spirit descends upon you, what should you do? Well, for starters, get out of the temple!' Translation: "get out of the way!"

His glory is meant to transform how we see life, people, work, our ministry, and our business. It aims to move us out of the way and place us where His rivers flow; it seeks to shift us from an earthly perspective to a spiritual one.

I also noticed in the verses mentioned above that the priests didn't complain or whine! No one was saying, "Where did this ugly smoke come from?" Or "Why do we have to leave our ministry?" Or "We haven't even gotten to the slow worship songs yet!"

When He arrives, what we need to prepare for is the wind of change. Our attitude should be like that of someone sailing in a small boat: "The wind is picking up, so let us hoist the sails and let this favorable wind carry us along at its speed."

All change begins with His glory; when we invite His glory into the temple, His power will follow! Neh'enah.

28

Why Walk When You Can Soar?

"Have you not known?
Have you not heard?
The everlasting God, the Lord,
The Creator of the ends of the earth,
Neither faints nor is weary.
His understanding is unsearchable.
He gives power to the weak,
And to those who have no might He increases strength.
Even the youths shall faint and be weary,
And the young men shall utterly fall,
But those who wait on the Lord
Shall renew their strength;
They shall mount up with wings like eagles,
They shall run and not be weary,
They shall walk and not faint." (Isaiah 40:28-31)

What a fantastic time to be alive and excited for the year ahead. The New Year has started, bringing high hopes, promises, goals, and new projects. Have you made your resolutions, set your new goals, and are you excited about all the possibilities? I am!

As I reflected on this past year's goals and challenges, I started to think more deeply about our life cycles and how we experience both good times and tough times. Our circumstances may change, but our determination to keep going must always stay strong.

There are things that happened this year I can explain; yet there are things around me that I cannot. Amid all this, I am being tested and proven. I am aware of the Lord's work in me and around me. Some things I loved, and some I would rather not repeat. Yet, as one of my mentors once said when facing difficulties and countless adversities in life: "So what?! I must arise and do what I'm supposed to do!"

Our lives change and evolve every day, whether we notice it or not. An ongoing transformation occurs both inside and outside of us. We need to understand this.

Now here's another important point to understand, as the writer of the Book of Hebrews beautifully expresses it: **"Remember your leaders and superiors in authority** [for it was they] **who brought to you the Word of God. Observe attentively and consider their way of living (the result of their well-spent lives) and imitate their faith (their conviction that God exists and is the Creator and Ruler of all things, the Provider and Bestower of eternal salvation through Christ, and their complete reliance on God in absolute trust and confidence in His power, wisdom, and goodness). Jesus Christ (the Messiah) is [always] the same, yesterday, today, [yes] and forever (to the ages)."** (Hebrews 13:7-8 Amplified Version)

People, situations, and circumstances may change – but Jesus Christ stays the same! He never changes; you can always depend on Him.

Last year's achievements and setbacks likely served their purpose, whether positive or negative. No matter how they impacted us emotionally, mentally, spiritually, or physically, we must move on quickly and turn our hearts back to Jesus Christ, who never changes!

As the Scripture mentioned above reads, **"Those who wait upon the Lord..."** it indicates that some, not all, will wait upon the Lord. Those who do will renew their strength, while those who don't will grow weak and fall.

As you start a new year, I encourage you to direct your affection toward things above rather than earthly things; I invite you to trust in the Lord and renew your strength so you can soar like the eagles!

Regarding the past or things you couldn't or wouldn't do, learn from them and move forward. Welcome a new day with excitement! As I mentioned in my title, "Why walk, when you can soar?! Neh'enah.

29

The Barnabas Anointing
Networking in the Kingdom?

"And when Saul had come to Jerusalem, he tried to join the disciples; but they were all afraid of him, and did not believe that he was a disciple. But Barnabas took him and brought him to the apostles. And he declared to them how he had seen the Lord on the road, and that He had spoken to him, and how he had preached boldly at Damascus in the name of Jesus." (Acts 9:26-27)

I love this testimony of how Saul of Tarsus, right after his own conversion to Christ, was unable to join the disciples of Jesus because they were afraid of him.

I'm sure the disciples were saying among themselves, "There is no way Saul could have gotten saved!" After all, they knew Saul from his wicked Christian-bashing years. They knew of his zeal to persecute the church, not to mention putting many in jail.

Can you relate to this? How can someone so evil now be praising the Lord Jesus Christ among the Christian community?! We who believe know that in Christ, all things are made new, but...

Although Saul had a miraculous conversion, Christ's followers required more; they needed someone they could trust before fully accepting Saul into the faith.

My friends, this is where networking plays a crucial role. Networking is about building bridges to support others' growth. Without Barnabas, Saul would have stayed on the sidelines during the Lord's movement in his time.

As I read my Bible and learn about the story in Acts, I'm amazed at how God orchestrated everything. But if I didn't know this story and I were living in the days of Saul of Tarsus, would I trust him without someone to vouch for him? Probably not. In fact, I know I wouldn't!

I once heard a man say, "No one succeeds alone." This wasn't a religious statement but a practical truth that encourages progress in any part of life. How many Barnabas-like people have you had in your life?

Look at where you are—it was all because someone stirred your heart, either pushed you, challenged you, or simply threw you into it! Have you been a "Barnabas" to someone? How many people have you challenged or walked alongside so they could experience a greater revelation or seize a better opportunity for growth?

I believe that as we continue with the Lord, our hearts will become more aware of this "Barnabas" anointing. We will soon see that we can't serve Jesus effectively alone. We need others in our lives to make it all happen. Together, with the right people, we can potentially achieve everything God has planned for us.

Here are two things to consider and reflect on deeply: 1) recognize how others have helped us along the way, and 2) are we doing the same for others? Neh'enah.

30

Detached! Part 1

"Do not love or cherish the world or the things that are in the world. If anyone loves the world, love for the Father is not in him." (1 John 2:15 AMP)

In this Scripture passage I am referencing, lexicographers define the word "world" [Gr.] Kosmos, as the worldly order that is separate from God, rebelled against Him and was condemned by both nature and godless actions.

The beloved disciple John guides us into God's heart and reveals His advice not to love or cherish the world or its possessions. Does this need more explanation? Probably not – but think about why John took the time to mention it.

I believe that what John refers to here is very different from what we have heard preached, taught, or mentioned in many pulpits today. People tend to judge by outward appearances and make snap judgments. Most have no idea what a "world order or system" really means.

I remember the day when a friend of mine told me that at a certain church, the ushers were carrying around measuring tapes to make sure that the sister's skirts were six inches below the knee. I'm not saying that's a bad thing, but I do believe that "worldliness" is more than just a short skirt and tattoos.

An Anti-Christ Spirit is a Worldly System

The world, as I mentioned in my devotion today, is a system of corruption. It's a world that defiles anything holy and divine. It promotes rebellion and exalts itself against the mind of Christ. If you find yourself thinking unwholesome thoughts or promoting yourself instead of Christ, you might be as "worldly" as they come.

Now, you might say, "Pastor Dave, I gave my life to Jesus ten years ago!" So what? Judas followed Jesus face-to-face for three years and in the end betrayed Him! Don't tell me that your "Christian" label is going to protect you from the worldly system that is out to get you.

The "world" as John uses it is a system that constantly tries to grab your attention, trap you, control you, and then destroy you! The believer must always remain sober and alert so they can recognize when contamination is near.

Every Backslider Starts Slow

Anyone who declares Jesus Christ as Lord is not immune to falling away from Him. You might believe that you'll never betray Christ; you might tell yourself and others, "I love God so much that I would never walk away from Him!" However, in your arrogance, you could stumble.

No one falls away on a specific day. The falling away starts when the "anti-Christ spirit" begins to pull you aside little by little. It seeps into your mind and then your heart, and finally, you end up back in the world from which Christ brought you out! Before you know it, you're without peace, without joy, and full of shame.

Every backslider begins gradually. Sin isn't committed openly at first, but it increases as it is entertained in the mind. This is something we must keep on our spiritual radar, and once we recognize it, we must detach from it. Neh'enah.

31

Detached! Part 2

"For all that is in the world—the lust of the flesh [craving for sensual gratification] **and the lust of the eyes** [greedy longings of the mind] **and the pride of life** [assurance in one's own resources or in the stability of earthly things]—**these do not come from the Father but are from the world** [itself]. **And the world passes away and disappears, and with it the forbidden cravings (the passionate desires, the lust) of it; but he who does the will of God and carries out His purposes in his life abides (remains) forever."** (1 John 2:16-17 AMP)

As a young believer, our pastor consistently emphasized the importance of following Jesus. He spoke against sin, disobedience, and anything that opposed the gospel of the kingdom, but mainly, he focused on teaching us to follow Jesus.

In other words, he would put God's will before our own.

In the Holiness Movement, many sought a pure life but took no action toward God's work, resulting in a stagnant life — one that didn't carry the presence of Jesus anywhere.

Many of those followers, in pursuit of perfection, ended up criticizing and tearing each other apart. The very thing Paul warned against in Galatians.

The message of holiness is a declaration: "I want all that Jesus has for me!" It's not just about overcoming sin but also about stepping into the harvest Jesus called us to.

The Lord is calling us to cleanse ourselves from our flesh and perfect ourselves in holiness, while also doing His will by touching lives for Him. I remember in my early days of walking with Jesus, there was a particular hymn that so touched my soul and still makes me fall in love with Him over and over again.

Turn your eyes upon Jesus
look full in His wonderful face
and the things of earth will grow strangely dim
in the light of His glory and grace

Turn your eyes upon Jesus
look full in His wonderful face
and the things of earth will grow strangely dim
in the light of His glory and grace.

My dear friends, detach yourselves from worldly possessions. Focus your hearts on things above, as Paul clearly states in Colossians 3. Pursue God's will; clothe yourselves with Christ, and the things of earth will fade in the light of His glory and grace! Neh'enah.

32

When God Stops Your Party!

"Again David gathered all the choice men of Israel, thirty thousand. And David arose and went with all the people who were with him from Baale Judah to bring up from there the ark of God, whose name is called by the Name, the Lord of Hosts, who dwells between the cherubim. So they set the ark of God on a new cart, and brought it out of the house of Abinadab, which was on the hill; and Uzzah and Ahio, the sons of Abinadab, drove the new cart. And they brought it out of the house of Abinadab, which was on the hill, accompanying the ark of God; and Ahio went before the ark. Then David and all the house of Israel played music before the Lord on all kinds of instruments of fir wood, on harps, on stringed instruments, on tambourines, on sistrums, and on cymbals. And when they came to Nachon's threshing floor, Uzzah put out his hand to the ark of God and took hold of it, for the oxen stumbled. Then the anger of the Lord was aroused against Uzzah, and God struck him there for his error; and he died there by the ark of God. And David became angry because of the Lord's outbreak against Uzzah; and he called the name of the place Perez Uzzah to this day." (2 Samuel 6:1-8)

Have you ever noticed this powerful story in the Bible —the one about David bringing the Ark of the Covenant back to Jerusalem? It serves as a testament to the Lord's divine order in matters concerning His will.

I believe that God wanted the Ark of the Covenant in Jerusalem; I believe He placed this desire in David's heart, and David was determined to bring it home. It wasn't that it wasn't God's will to get it, but the reverence in how it was brought back had everything to do with fulfilling God's will His way!

Regarding God's will in this story, God had already chosen the only ones who would carry this sacred piece of furniture. Not everyone in the camp was allowed to carry or touch it. Listen to this: **"And when Aaron and his sons have finished covering the sanctuary and all the furnishings of the sanctuary, when the camp is set to go, then the sons of Kohath shall come to carry them; but they shall not touch any holy thing, lest they die."** (Numbers 4:15)

God had given specific orders about who should cover the furniture and who would be the only ones to carry it. Apparently, this divine order had been ignored, and the obvious happened! Someone had to die for the party to stop!

God loves worship —understand me —but divine order must always be the standard for all followers of Christ. Our lives and ministries are full of singing, dancing, and clapping, but lack divine order. I mean, does it matter if you sing in the name of the Lord if your life is out of God's order? Think about it.

Here's what I've learned from my own life about this revelation: there are reasons why judgment comes our way and temporarily pauses us. I also want to point out that things don't just happen overnight — there is a spiritual decline that eventually leads to judgment. Here is the sequence of that decline and how it develops in our hearts.

1. Flippant – The term 'flippant' describes being dismissively disrespectful, shallow, or lacking seriousness. Becoming flippant truly starts when someone loses connection with God. Once we begin to grow cold in our prayer life or set aside God's Word, a spirit of flippancy can creep in, if you will. We start to lower our standards, and suddenly we become less serious about what we once considered holy and divine.

2. Careless – The definition is not paying enough attention to what one

does. Once the seriousness of a thing is gone, we start "dropping the ball" on things we used to value. We still pay attention, but it is no longer front and center, as it once was.

3. Neglect or Negligent – Lastly, we have the word negligent. A negligent individual is someone who pays little or no attention to something or disregards it entirely. Once a person becomes flippant in attitude and careless about their "known" responsibilities, then negligence becomes unavoidable! This is what I believe happened to King David. We can all focus on the outward and end up neglecting the inward!

This is what I believe sometimes happens to all truly faithful, God-seeking individuals. Aligning our lives to please God is not an easy task. There is a constant awareness that must always be active on our part. Neh'enah.

33

What Is Your Soul's First Necessity?

"THE SPIRIT of God came upon Azariah son of Oded. And he went out to meet Asa and said to him, Hear me, Asa, and all Judah and Benjamin: the Lord is with you while you are with Him. If you seek Him [inquiring for and of Him, craving Him as your soul's first necessity], He will be found by you; but if you [become indifferent and] forsake Him, He will forsake you." (2 Chronicles 15:1, 2)

"The acts of Asa, from first to last, are written in the Book of the Kings of Judah and Israel. In the thirty-ninth year of his reign Asa was diseased in his feet—until his disease became very severe; yet in his disease he did not seek the Lord, but relied on the physicians. And Asa slept with his fathers, dying in the forty-first year of his reign." (2 Chronicles 16:11-13)

Have you ever been somewhere where you felt deep inside that something was missing? Something beyond logic and natural order (like status, reputation, financial stability, or great success), yet you knew what was once there was no longer present? What is this emotion, and what does it reveal about the human spirit?

The discomfort of this feeling or emotion occurs when the Fountain of Life (Jesus, the Lord) stops supplying fresh water, and an endless thirst begins to consume you.

If the emotion is set aside, the temptation will be to replace it with something else. Many who have walked with the Lord have experienced this sad but true reality. The sense of overwhelming darkness and loneliness that comes when the Fountain no longer produces the freshness of life within you; indeed, then a choice must be made.

Life or Death: It's My Choice

Many have gone through this in their walk with God, and if you haven't experienced it yet, you will! It is inevitable to face the rebellion of our old nature in life, which tries to take over and regain the ground lost to everyone walking in the power of the Holy Spirit.

The choice is really yours! You can decide to live by the Spirit of God and succeed, or you will fall into fleshly desires and eventually face spiritual decline and corruption. All of us will go through this!

Dealing with Indifference

The Scripture I referenced above speaks about the Prophet Azariah. This man of God came to encourage and exhort King Asa. He basically told him that if he made Jehovah his life's passion and the priority of his soul, he would be found by God at every turn. He guaranteed King Asa victory if he always sought the Lord. What a promise! What a guarantee!

I'm not exactly sure what happened or when, but King Asa lost his way. In his thirty-ninth year as king, he developed an illness in his feet. The Scripture says that even then, he didn't seek the Lord but trusted in his physicians. Wow! Isn't that something? He died two years later—away from the Lord, I believe.

God-Led Leadership!

What happens to our leadership? Our leadership functions without God, but it falls far short of its true potential when God isn't guiding our hearts. No matter what kind of enterprise you're leading — whether it's an organization, church, ministry, business, family, or team — you would be in a much better state of conscience if you recognized that the Lord is the One leading you at every step.

I want to leave you with this thought: God will always lift up the humble and contrite and make a way for them; but if the humble become proud and arrogant, God's favor will disappear just as quickly as it came! Neh'enah.

34

The Wonder of An Open Heart!

"Now a certain woman named Lydia heard us. She was a seller of purple from the city of Thyatira, who worshiped God. The Lord opened her heart to heed the things spoken by Paul. And when she and her household were baptized..." (Acts 16:14-15a)

As I meditated on this one passage of Scripture and recounted Paul's visit to Philippi, I was once again reminded by the Holy Spirit that God will use us as instruments wherever we go.

Paul and his group attended a prayer meeting by the riverside where some women gathered to pray. It was here that Paul met Lydia. He could have met others, but for some reason, Lydia stood out. Why? She stood out because her heart was open and she paid attention to what Paul said. This made all the difference!

Many have come "in the name of the Lord," but failed to open their hearts to His true purpose. This is the real problem in our religious world, called Christianity. We tend to falter by accepting that people "show up" for a meeting rather than genuinely opening their hearts to understand God's wisdom for their lives.

Have you opened your heart to the Spirit of God lately? What is He saying? Do you feel a prompting in the atmosphere where you attend church, hold prayer meetings, or read your own Bible at home? Everything about God depends on having an open heart toward Him!

Here is what I have learned when my heart has been opened to God and I have listened to the words spoken to my spirit.

1. Revelation. The Spirit of revelation or a greater revelation of the person of Jesus Christ increases within me. I am quickened and made aware of His knowledge and what He truly expects from me. It is a glorious experience to open our hearts to God and pay attention to what He is saying.

2. Freshness. A freshness in my spirit overtakes me when God visits my open heart. A freshness is like a cup of cold water to a weary soul in a dry and thirsty land. Dryness occurs when flesh controls our decision-making process. Ministry, working, serving, helping, reaching out, and many other good works are the culprits for drying up our souls. That is why a freshness is necessary.

3. God's Will Rekindled. When we become consumed with ourselves, our ministry, our jobs, or our business, we tend to believe that this is the only way to live. What we might not realize is that these things, as valuable as they are, can become obstacles to experiencing the fresh and revelatory will of God for us.

As I close, remember: Just because things seem to be going well doesn't mean God is for it. When we open our hearts to God's voice, we will discover in greater fullness what He is really saying to us now! Neh'enah.

35

Will You Worship?

"Now there was a day when his sons and daughters were eating and drinking wine in their oldest brother's house; and a messenger came to Job and said, "The oxen were plowing and the donkeys feeding beside them, when the Sabeans raided them and took them away—indeed they have killed the servants with the edge of the sword; and I alone have escaped to tell you!" While he was still speaking, another also came and said, "The fire of God fell from heaven and burned up the sheep and the servants, and consumed them; and I alone have escaped to tell you!" While he was still speaking, another also came and said, "The Chaldeans formed three bands, raided the camels and took them away, yes, and killed the servants with the edge of the sword; and I alone have escaped to tell you!" While he was still speaking, another also came and said, "Your sons and daughters were eating and drinking wine in their oldest brother's house, and suddenly a great wind came from across the wilderness and struck the four corners of the house, and it fell on the young people, and they are dead; and I alone have escaped to tell you! Then Job arose, tore his robe, and shaved his head; and he fell to the ground and worshiped. And he said: "Naked I came from my mother's womb, And naked shall I return there. The LORD gave, and the LORD has taken away; Blessed be the name of the LORD." (Job 1:13-21)

Reading the story of Job has been both inspiring and challenging.

As the writer tells us, Job was blameless and upright, and outwardly or materially speaking, Job had all his "ducks in line." What wrong could possibly happen to a man who is one step ahead of everyone else? What negative thing could come upon a man who is always thinking positively? Or what wicked adversity could come upon a man who is so close to God that God Himself considers him – special?!

The life story of Job as depicted in Scripture is a message for passionate worshippers of God. It is not a message for those seeking a "bed of roses" or an easy way to serve Jesus! No sir. The message of Job is for those who desire to be broken, challenged, and allowed to be rebuilt in a more refined way!

Stripped!

Much of what we hear being taught in our Christian circles today rarely addresses subjects like brokenness, dying to self, living in the Spirit, and following Jesus with full-hearted devotion. For some, "walking in the Spirit" means an opportunity to act and behave strangely. It's funny to me how they don't behave that way in public!

One thing I know: When Paul was knocked off his horse, finally regained his eyesight, and was filled with God's power, he went out and changed the world. Today, we stumble, get up, and head to our favorite restaurant, like a steakhouse, to process the religious experience. What?! No action?! The following week, we return to the same place seeking another dose of spiritual experience, but there's no brokenness—no action. Until when? No wonder the world mocks the church!

Job was a man full of blessings, with a good reputation and seemingly responsible in following Jehovah. Everything was going smoothly until... until God decided to unleash His fire into Job's life.

The man who was once respected by all is now losing everything God gave him. One thing after another: his cattle, his servants, his children— all of it taken away by the mighty hand of the Lord! I don't know about you, but this is a heavy trial in Job's life. How much can a man endure? You might be surprised.

Will You Worship?

Once everything was taken away, Job still had to make a choice. His landscape was different, his checkbook was empty, his cattle had been stolen, his dear children gone — it was all gone! What did Job have left? He had a small fire in his spirit that refused to be extinguished by external circumstances.

Listen to the last few lines of this chapter: **Then Job arose, tore his robe, and shaved his head; and he fell to the ground and worshiped. And he said: "Naked I came from my mother's womb, and naked shall I return there. The LORD gave, and the LORD has taken away; Blessed be the name of the LORD."**

Though Job was broken and shattered, he remained unwavering! Job was forced to re-evaluate everything he had — his faith, his material possessions, his calling, and every circumstance surrounding him at that moment. Through it all, Job continued to worship!

A Deeper Philosophy of Life

"Naked I came from my mother's womb and naked shall I return there. The Lord gave, and the Lord has taken away; blessed by the name of the Lord." (Job 1:21)

I've heard people quote this Scripture when facing tough times; the only difference is they haven't gone through what Job experienced. They may have lost a few things, but they still hold onto their secret stash of possessions, family, and contacts. Job lost everything! E-v-e-r-y-t-h-i-n-g!

When Job said this, he truly meant it! Job understood that all things come from God. He wasn't fixated on materialism. He wasn't concerned with reputation! He didn't care what anyone thought of him. He knew the Source of his future was God! He simply entrusted himself faithfully to Him who was able to deliver him in the end. Neh'enah.

36

Are You Putting New Upholstery in the Titanic?

"Look after each other so that none of you fails to receive the grace of God. Watch out that no poisonous root of bitterness grows up to trouble you, corrupting many." (Hebrews 12:15)

I recently came across this Scripture when I had the chance to meet with a few friends to talk about an ongoing issue with a dear brother. This brother wanted to share and open his heart to receive counsel while also trying to align himself with God's will. It was a very interesting meeting, to say the least.

A Person's World Flows from the Heart

I have always believed and was taught early on that all of life's issues originate from the heart. Here is what Proverbs says about this:

"Watch over your heart with all diligence, for from it flow the springs of life." (Proverbs 4:23 - NAS)

"Be careful how you think; your life is shaped by your thoughts." (Proverbs 4:23 - Good News Translation)

"Guard your heart more than anything else, because the source of your life flows from it." (Proverbs 4:23 - GOD'S WORD Translation)

As I listened to my dear brother speak and share his heart with us, I quickly sensed the Holy Spirit say to me, "He is bitter. Very bitter!" After hearing God's voice, I realized that the man was consumed by unforgiveness, which has led to bitterness and hatred.

Other advice came from others in response to this dear brother's heart-break; I knew this man had been hiding behind shallow Christian teachings and sermons that provoke the mind but not the heart! As I listened along with the others, my heart began to burn within me, and I spoke out. I said, "My dear brother, you have a major issue that has you trapped – it is called unforgiveness, which has brought much bitterness to your soul. You must repent and turn to God, so He can heal you and restore your life. Then you will have a better view of life than you have now. Nothing will happen "around you" until it "happens within you!"

Others who were present looked at me as if I were out of my mind or as if I had come from another planet.

You Can't Fix Externals Until Internals Are Fixed!

One thing I see increasing in our churches today is this: people try to fix personal sin issues with good (philosophical) ideas. Psychology can't fix a sin problem. Psychology may work, but only once a man has been restored to his original place in God. Otherwise, it's like putting new upholstery on the Titanic!

Remember that the world fell under a curse because of the sin of disobedience. Disobedience brought shame, pain, and guilt to man, which he now faces. It caused a separation from God and left man to live by his own strength.

The root of man's countless problems is his selfishness; he desires to control his own life and has a passion to know what he doesn't know and can't know. Unless man turns to God by accepting Christ's redemption plan, he will continue to wander in pain and despair.

Self is the poison that destroys us all. This brother I've been talking about needs to first receive forgiveness from God, then forgive himself, then forgive those who have wronged him, and finally pray for the people (his enemies) he hates – yes, in that order.

I have never been a fan of quick-fix formulas, but this one is guaranteed to work if approached with humility and a contrite heart. I'm not a licensed counselor or doctor, but I genuinely believe that this "formula" will resolve the problem faster than any depression medication or therapy anyone might be receiving. Neh'enah.

37

To Die For!

"And see, now I go bound in the spirit to Jerusalem, not knowing the things that will happen to me there, except that the Holy Spirit testifies in every city, saying that chains and tribulations await me. But none of these things move me; nor do I count my life dear to myself, so that I may finish my race with joy, and the ministry which I received from the Lord Jesus, to testify to the gospel of the grace of God." (Acts 20:22-24)

When I consider the purpose and vision behind a man's philosophy, I also question the passion and fire driving that person's willingness to pursue their plan at any cost. In some cases, people literally die for their cause.

Now, I have also come across many people who say they have a great vision and a strong purpose—to become an agent of change, a world-changer if you will—and to contribute in a meaningful way to society and the world at large. However, they often never actually get there. I'm sure there are many reasons why some contribute a lot, while others never reach this coveted place of impact.

I want to share a few observations as we continue pursuing our dream and fulfilling what we believe God has put in our hearts.

Key 1: For one thing is certain, a man or woman of vision must have a vision that is bigger than life itself! The vision must be much larger than what they currently are! Vision is not just a collection of ideas you gather from reading a magazine or attending a conference or seminar – no sir, a vision is the ability to see with the eyes of the heart. See a picture so vivid that it can literally stress you out. In the spirit, there is perfect peace, but in the natural, there is a stirring that stresses you out and keeps you awake.

Key 2: Another important principle regarding vision is that it often is the very thing that keeps you focused and fine-tuned in your endeavors. With vision, you will know where to spend your time, money, and efforts. Without the ability to see, you will shoot at everything all the time – but hit nothing; you will become a "chaser of rabbits," and never catch one! - an individual who becomes the "jack of all trades but master of none!" I have met too many individuals who live their lives at the mercy of others. They have placed their entire future in the hands of someone else!

Key 3: This key might be the real motivation behind great achievement. Are you willing to die for your vision? Are you willing to die "on the hill" of your God-given dream? I believe this is the main difference between most would-be visionaries and others; some will die for it, and some will give up. One thing I've noticed about passionate people is this – they will reach their goal, or they will die trying! How close are you to doing this for your own vision?

In closing this entry, I want to say that the Apostle Paul loved Jesus, and he demonstrated this through his sincere obedience to the Lord—obedience that so powerfully touched Him and reached out to him on the road to Damascus. He wasn't just spouting spiritual talk, making countless foolish confessions, or even trying to impress his fellow Christians. Listen to this: **"Then Paul answered, "What do you mean by weeping and breaking my heart? For I am ready not only to be bound, but also to die at Jerusalem for the name of the Lord Jesus.'"** (Acts 21:13)

Paul believed in the gospel of Jesus Christ; Paul lived as someone indebted to the gospel; Paul suffered greatly for the gospel of Jesus Christ, and finally, this great man of God, Paul, literally died for the gospel of Jesus Christ!

Listen to Paul's heart: **"This is why I suffer as I do. Still, I am not ashamed; for I know Him** [and I am personally acquainted with Him] **whom I have believed** [with absolute trust and confidence in Him and in the truth of

His deity], **and I am persuaded** [beyond any doubt] **that He is able to guard what I have entrusted to Him until that day** [when I stand before Him]. (2 Timothy 1:12 *Amplified Version*) Neh'enah.

38

When God Plays Checkers!

Look, I go forward, but He is not there, and backward, but I cannot perceive Him;
When He works on the left hand, I cannot behold Him;
When He turns to the right hand, I cannot see Him.
But He knows the way that I take;
When He has tested me, I shall come forth as gold." (Job 23:8-10)

I heard a man once ask the question: "Who is sending all these trials upon my life? God or the Devil?" Another man stood up and answered, "It doesn't really matter who is testing you; what matters is how you are reacting to the trials in your life!"

I have to say this is one of the wisest answers I have heard in a long time. To put it in perspective and with some theological balance, Job was tested by the Lord and used the devil to do the dirty work, if you can call it that. God trusted Job and allowed him to face the fire of adversity in many ways.

I know that today, with all the watered-down theology about suffering and adversity, people tend to believe that all "bad things" come from Satan and all "good things" come from the Lord. As reasonable as that sounds, it is not actually true.

The Lord is King over all; even the devil is under His authority. You must never forget that! When we enter God's kingdom, we become His servants and submit to the will of the King. I am currently a servant under the lordship of King Jesus, and nothing can affect my life unless my King allows it. I am to submit myself and follow God's vision and purpose for my life. There is no greater plan for my life than to walk in God's divine order.

In the story of Job, God tested him and permitted the devil to do so. It was a very difficult and challenging test for Job. One thing to note, and as a word of encouragement to everyone facing heavy adversity: the devil was on a leash! He could touch everything outside of Job's life, but he could not harm his internal life.

Job had a wife and four friends who came to offer him words of encouragement and wisdom, but to no avail. That is what happens when God is working in us—no one can truly help us reach where we need to be with God. Only a revelation of Jesus Christ will bring us to that place where God calls us to be.

As Job pondered and carefully thought about his current situation, he was convinced that if he could just find God, he could make his case before Him. The only problem was—God was hiding from him. Job couldn't find God anywhere!

In the Scripture above, Job was essentially saying, "I know God is moving all around me, but I can't find Him!" Doesn't this sound like us at times? Our lives are being moved around like a checker on a checkerboard, and we don't know where or when the next move will be!

Then Job concludes the matter and reaches a place where he stops seeking answers, resting upon the Lord, and says, **"But He knows the way that I take; when He has tested me, I shall come forth as gold."**

You and I will face many challenges; we will do our best to find answers: we will blame Satan, we will blame God, we will blame our leaders, we will blame our government, we will blame everyone—and all to no avail.

Then, finally, we will arrive at the place where we 'settle down" and recognize that God is King over our lives. He reserves the right to lead us in the best way possible. This is where we learn to trust Him and say with Job, "**... when He has tested me, I shall come forth as gold.'** Neh'enah.

39

Take Care of a Few Simple Things First!

"Do you not know that you are God's Sanctuary, and that the Spirit of God has His home within you?" (1 Corinthians 3:16) Weymouth New Testament

As the year keeps moving forward and many of our goals continue to unfold, we often find ourselves needing an extra push or encouragement to reach the next level of achievement or performance.

One thing I have noticed about those who are driven by a fire within is that they will not settle for anything less than what their spiritual eyes have seen. As we are led by the Spirit of God, we are often challenged by a big giant – SELF!

Here's my true feeling about the greatest enemy we face: He lives within us twenty-four hours a day, three hundred sixty-five days a year. He never sleeps or slumbers either and often waits for us to procrastinate, neglect, or simply give up on our God-given purpose.

You know exactly who I'm talking about, yes, our flesh – the enemy within. The one that's been challenging us ever since we entered the glorious kingdom of God.

Knowing that our flesh opposes all that is holy and divine, we must especially ensure that we tend to the basics; the exercises that help our lives thrive with joy and excitement.

There are many things we can do that make us happy, but only a few things truly excite us spiritually and give us the feeling of accomplishment and progress!

When I talk about exercises, I'm not referring to twenty different activities just to feel good. I'm talking about tending to three necessities:

1. Our prayer life is the one key practice that will strengthen your spirit man or inner man. It will be the key to understanding what God is thinking, saying, and doing. If you become someone who longs to understand the heart of God, prayer is the path to that understanding.

2. Our Study Life. Becoming a student of life by reading materials that will enable you and make you a better man or woman is the key to building your mind and soul. God's Word is one precious book you want to take notes on! Don't be an idiot by default. We must continue to train our minds in the things that better equip us for God's purposes. This is an area we cannot afford to neglect. What we don't know will hurt us!

3. Our Physical Exercise. The body is the only machine we have. Every dream and desire is lived through this one body. It must be taken care of. Doing natural exercises and going for long walks are very healthy for your cardio and muscles; not to mention the benefit of releasing stress. Can you imagine having many dreams, plans, ambitions, and goals - but no body available that you can use to live out these God-given blessings?!

As I close this chapter, I want to encourage you to rise in the name of the Lord! It doesn't matter where you have been in your past; what matters is that you focus on the basics starting today. Leave all the complicated stuff for the overly smart ones; you achieve your dreams by taking care of a few simple things. Neh'enah.

40

Dreams: God's Way of By-Passing Your Intellect!

"For God may speak in one way, or in another, yet man does not perceive it. In a dream, in a vision of the night, when deep sleep falls upon men, while slumbering on their beds, then He opens the ears of men, and seals their instruction." (Job 33:14-16)

When I read this portion of Scripture, many experiences I've had with God come to mind. One of those experiences is how He has guided me in my calling and through difficult transitional phases in my life.

Now, as I write this, I'm also very aware that I didn't always understand what God was doing. Sometimes, I felt more lost than ever. Just because we walk with God doesn't mean we always perceive what He is saying and doing. In fact, God can be pretty mysterious at times.

Here's one thing I've learned: God will always show up at your crossroads. "Never late, seldom early, but always on time!" to quote my spiritual mentor.

Dreams of God

Every dream we have comes from the Lord. As crazy and mysterious as the dream might be, God is speaking loudly and clearly to our hearts. Some might think that dreams occur because of a heavy dinner before sleep – and while this may be true for some, most of us dream the dreams of God.

Dreams are God's language in the night. He speaks to our subconscious and quickens our hearts by provoking us to seek Him hard. Once we are

108

provoked to find out what a dream means, God will bring in the people who can interpret the mystery for us.

Why a Dream?

God knows our fleshly weaknesses and tendencies. He knows very well that we are intelligent human beings and that we tend to rely on human reasoning most of the time. So, when God is trying to get our attention on any subject and He really needs us to "get it," He will bypass our natural reasoning and go straight into our hearts or subconscious to reveal His wishes to us! Isn't this amazing? In this way, we don't have the chance to criticize, judge, ignore, neglect, or reject "the Messenger."

If an individual, such as a pastor or prophet of the Lord, etc., spoke to us and gave us a much-needed word from God, we could easily tell him, "Ok, thank you for the Word; I'll be praying about it." And then do nothing with that word! However, when God releases a dream full of prophetic instruction, our attitude would be different. Our hearts and minds would be captivated; we would be compelled to dwell on that powerful emotion.

As I finish these notes, ask God to speak to you through dreams first. Then, pray to receive the gift of interpreting dreams. As God begins to send prophetic dreams your way, start writing them down—keep a journal. By taking notes, God will help clarify your future through these dreams. One thing I know for sure: God will speak to you if you ask Him to. Neh'enah.

41

Soldiers Under Command! Part 1

"Then she said to him, "How can you say, 'I love you,' when your heart is not with me? You have mocked me these three times and have not told me where your great strength lies." And it came to pass, when she pestered him daily with her words and pressed him, so that his soul was vexed to death, that he told her all his heart, and said to her, "No razor has ever come upon my head, for I have been a Nazirite to God from my mother's womb. If I am shaven, then my strength will leave me, and I shall become weak, and be like any other man." (Judges 16:15-17)

One of the most interesting stories I have read is found in the Book of Judges. It's the story of Samson and Delilah. If you have never read the whole story, it's a must-read for anyone who aspires to be a leader, a business owner, or a minister of God's Word.

If you have ever read the Book of Judges, it's mainly a historical account of how Israel rebelled against the Lord after entering the Promised Land. As they went deeper into the land, opposition kept increasing, and the battles became more intense. By this time, Joshua had died; God-ordained leadership was at an all-time low. When authentic God-ordained leadership is missing, the people tend to stray.

As I was writing this, I started thinking about the mentors I have had in my life over the years. I have learned a lot from all of them, and I am deeply grateful for everything God has brought into my life to help me grow and develop my skills. Some of my mentors were wonderful and served as living testimonies of God's keeping power; others faced loss and failure in their business or ministry. I have learned from the good, the bad, and the ugly!

Joshua was a great man of God, and the Lord used Him to finish what Moses had started. Yet, it seems that Joshua didn't really prepare anyone to lead after his death. Maybe he wasn't supposed to, but chances are he was supposed to train someone and did not. Whatever the case, it was what it was. The Hebrew children now had to deal with changing times—Joshua is dead!

It was at this stage of their conquest when the Hebrew children went to battle, but as it happens in any war - without proper leadership, progress becomes quite difficult and fulfilling any mission is almost impossible.

Many tribes in Canaan resisted leaving the land, and the Hebrew children lacked the leadership to remove them. So, what was the outcome? It was compromise. They compromised with the tribes, and if you must know, whenever there is any kind of compromise, you will end up doing what you are not supposed to do. This became the situation for the Hebrew children.

Like any form of compromise, all kinds of sin started to infiltrate the Hebrew camp, and God was displeased with all of it. It was then that God handed them over to their enemies, and the cycle of raising judges to lead Israel began.

The cycle of sin and repentance became a repeating pattern over the years. The pattern went like this: the people would sin; God would send an army to defeat them and take them into captivity; then God's people would cry out to the Lord in repentance, and God would rescue them by raising a judge. Once they were freed, a new order would be established. This cycle would continue for several years until they sinned again. Then the whole process would start over. It was a never-ending cycle.

As I conclude this first part, note some of the issues that typically challenge a man's leadership. It will always come down to matters of character.

If you are a leader, train others to become leaders. Also, understand that compromising will open the floodgates of ungodliness into your life. Any cycle of indulge, repent; indulge, repent; indulge, repent will ultimately hurt you in the long run. Neh'enah.

42

Soldiers Under Command! Part 2

"Then she said to him, "How can you say, 'I love you,' when your heart is not with me? You have mocked me these three times and have not told me where your great strength lies." And it came to pass, when she pestered him daily with her words and pressed him, so that his soul was vexed to death, that he told her all his heart, and said to her, "No razor has ever come upon my head, for I have been a Nazirite to God from my mother's womb. If I am shaven, then my strength will leave me, and I shall become weak, and be like any other man." (Judges 16:15-17)

Sampson, A Man Under Command

It came to pass that God heard the cry of the Hebrew children and raised a man named Samson. He was born out of barrenness, and his parents were instructed to dedicate their newborn son, Samson, to a Nazarite vow (Judges 13:2-5).

In the Hebrew Bible, a Nazirite or Nazarite is someone who voluntarily takes a vow described in Numbers 6:1-21. "Nazarite" derives from the Hebrew word נזיר nazir, meaning "consecrated" or "separated." This vow required the person to:

- Avoid wine, wine vinegar, grapes, raisins, intoxicating liquors, vinegar made from these, and consuming any items with traces of grapes.
- Refrain from cutting the hair on one's head; instead, allow the locks of hair to grow.
- Avoid becoming ritually impure through contact with corpses or graves, including those of family members.

The Battle Within!

One of the most captivating things I learned from the life of Sampson and truly admire is his zeal for the Lord. It was clear that this man had been touched and chosen by the Lord for His service. He was powerfully anointed! Yet, in Sampson's life, his real battle was not outward but inward.

Sampson had an insatiable desire for strange women. He had a heart full of lust, was extremely selfish, and took the call of God very lightly. All these characteristics created a recipe for disaster. Although he was mightily anointed, Sampson didn't walk in contriteness of heart. Here was a man who focused on the gifts of power but ignored the importance of character development through God's work within. Finally, the day arrived when the biggest trial of his life so far came upon him—the name of the trial was Delilah.

Was It Delilah's Fault?

All my Christian life, I have heard teachers, prophets, and pastors exhort the people to be very careful with temptation. Repeatedly, these devoted servants scold, threaten, and emphasize loudly to run away from the wickedness that surrounds them.

In my opinion, I have always felt that if the problem was external, all we had to do was move to a monastery and never peek out to see the world, and we would be fine if the problem is truly an external one! Who are we fooling?

The real issue here is that the problem lies within us. It is never external but internal. James said, **"But each one is tempted when he is drawn away by his own desires and enticed. Then, when desire has conceived, it gives birth to sin; and sin, when it is full-grown, brings forth death."** (James 1:14, 15)

The Law of Attraction is Real: Our Hearts are Magnets!

When you have a heart for Jesus, all kinds of good things come your way. When you pursue a life of prayer, things related to intimacy with God come your way. When you are in love with the King of Kings, revelations of who He is are revealed! Whatever is in your heart and mind—that is what you receive!

Now, for the negative side, it is also true. Our hearts are magnets! Whatever is in us is what we will attract. If lust is controlling our hearts, then lust is what we will encounter. If greed is in our hearts, then greed or opportunities to be greedy will be drawn to us.

You can't get what you're not! It's impossible to believe in something and receive the opposite of what you believe.

Your Heart Invites

Whatever you desire, you get! We could start debating whether Delilah was vicious and used as a stumbling block for the great Samson to fall, but for some reason I don't believe that was the case at all.

I believe Sampson, driven by his ego, lust, and desire for power, got what he truly wanted. The more he viewed it as a challenge to his ego, the more she kept returning. Delilah kept sticking around because Sampson wanted her there. He was only fulfilling his true desire — feeding his lust.

Delilah came to Sampson four times before Sampson lost the fear of the Lord and revealed the secret of his great strength. It wasn't that Delilah was stronger; it was because of Sampson's lack of contriteness and humility in his heart toward Jehovah God.

When humility left, pride surged like a tsunami. It was then that Sampson fell into the hands of the Philistines. Let your heart ponder this truth. Neh'enah.

43

Soldiers Under Command! Part 3

Then she said to him, "How can you say, 'I love you,' when your heart is not with me? You have mocked me these three times and have not told me where your great strength lies." And it came to pass, when she pestered him daily with her words and pressed him, so that his soul was vexed to death, that he told her all his heart, and said to her, "No razor has ever come upon my head, for I have been a Nazirite to God from my mother's womb. If I am shaven, then my strength will leave me, and I shall become weak, and be like any other man." (Judges 16:15-17)

The Results of Pride and Rebellion Toward the Spirit of God

Samson finally revealed the secret of his great power and opened his heart to a woman who, without doubt, had selfish intentions if not evil.

Once the Lord marks you to be all His, your life will never be the same. God will never let you get away with anything. You might try, but you won't get far. Men and women under command are special people in the Lord's sight. They are highly favored, if you will.

Persisting in rebellion against the Lord and His Spirit is never a good thing; in fact, rebellion will eventually cost us everything. It will take away all that God had planned for our destiny.

Here are a few things that one will miss if they persist in rebellion:

The loss of strength. Samson was quickly bound and taken captive. His actions had taken away the freedom he once had. He kept doing things his own way until "his own way" cost him everything valuable.

The loss of vision. Once in chains, captive to the Philistines, they gouged out his eyes. They took away his ability to see light! Nothing is more consequential to a man of God than losing his spiritual vision. The ability to see light was gone! This is very painful. And finally,

The loss of influence. Samson had become quite a household name in his day. People knew him and respected him. He was someone to the community and to Israel as a whole; but now, Samson had lost his name, his reputation, and his position in God. What a way to end a life!

As I end these few lines, I want to encourage you to rise from the ashes of discouragement and, in the name of Jesus, remember the purpose and destiny you have from the Lord.

Being caught in a battle due to rebellion is one thing, but being in a struggle for righteousness is different. The Spirit of God will reveal this to you, too. Meditate on it. Neh'enah.

44

Appreciative of Change!

"Now in the second month of the second year of their coming to the house of God at Jerusalem, Zerubbabel the son of Shealtiel, Jeshua the son of Jozadak, and the rest of their brethren the priests and the Levites, and all those who had come out of the captivity to Jerusalem, began work and appointed the Levites from twenty years old and above to oversee the work of the house of the LORD. Then Jeshua with his sons and brothers, Kadmiel with his sons, and the sons of Judah, arose as one to oversee those working on the house of God: the sons of Henadad with their sons and their brethren the Levites. When the builders laid the foundation of the temple of the LORD, the priests stood in their apparel with trumpets, and the Levites, the sons of Asaph, with cymbals, to praise the LORD, according to the ordinance of David king of Israel. And they sang responsively, praising and giving thanks to the LORD:
"For He is good,
For His mercy endures forever toward Israel."
Then all the people shouted with a great shout, when they praised the LORD, because the foundation of the house of the LORD was laid. But many of the priests and Levites and heads of the fathers' houses, old men who had seen the first temple, wept with a loud voice when the foundation of this temple was laid before their eyes. Yet many shouted aloud for joy, so that the people could not discern the noise of the shout of joy from the noise of the weeping of the people, for the people shouted with a loud shout, and the sound was heard afar off." (Ezra 3:8-13)

I was meditating on the words in the book of Ezra and discovered some very powerful and necessary wisdom. With that intent today, I want to share it with you so you can also be strengthened and understand how God directs and designs change in our lives.

An Old Mindset

Every time I read about the restoration of the temple in Jerusalem and its walls, I gain valuable insights into the mindset of those who experienced the transformation from the old temple to the newly remodeled one.

Rebuilding was a major accomplishment. Zerubbabel and his team of workers (those who came out of captivity) had dedicated themselves to rebuilding the temple. What an exciting time!

There seemed to be a desire to work and rebuild, and under proper leadership, the foundation was laid. This brought in the worship team to celebrate the work accomplished. It was truly a time to celebrate a new beginning.

What intrigues me is how some people get very excited about the possibilities and potential of a dream, while others don't. This new group of builders was so enthusiastic that they praised and sang unto the Lord for completing the first step in rebuilding God's glorious temple.

Not So Fast!

Apparently, some of the people helping with the reconstruction had seen the old temple before it was destroyed. Can you imagine that? They were not too fond of the new one.

"But many of the priests and Levites and heads of the fathers' houses, old men who had seen the first temple, wept with a loud voice when the foundation of this temple was laid before their eyes."

You might have expected these elders to be jumping for joy after the foundation was laid, but no! They started weeping. Why? I believe they began comparing the old with the new. This is rule number one: never compare yourself with your past. We all need to be mindful and focus on the progressiveness of God's work in us!

This is exactly what happens today in our walk with Jesus. The Lord begins a work in our lives, and because it doesn't align with our favorite self-made theology or past experiences, we abort the new work God is doing! There is something profound here.

Why can't people recognize the new things God is doing? Why is it so difficult to break free from tradition, ritualism, and the religious spirit in our lives?

Our Attitude Towards Change

Our attitude towards change will be very revealing, as our entire being will experience some form of shock in response to what needs to align with the present change.

We might feel joyful, sad, mad, confused, or delighted about our new-found opportunity for transformation.

When we are too close to a situation, we tend not to truly "get it." We are too near and need to step back a few paces to see all that God is doing. Once we shift our perspective and understand where we stand and what we are observing, we will deeply appreciate God's grace and plan.

Why Fear Has Paralyzed the Dreamer!

Nothing hampers the flow of the Lord in a believer's life like fear. Fear is a fruit of the flesh and can easily paralyze anyone who listens to it. Fear causes you to focus on yourself, not God; it makes you focus on your possessions, not what God can provide; it causes you to hear negativity instead of God's promise in the Spirit. Ultimately, fear will persuade you to follow a plan that can steal your destiny in God.

As I conclude these notes, reflect on your ways, your vision— the deposit of the call God has given you—and guard it with all your might. "**O Timothy, guard the deposit entrusted to you.**" (1 Timothy 6:20) Also, "**Guard the good treasure entrusted to you, with the help of the Holy Spirit who dwells in us.**" (2 Timothy 1:14) Neh'enah.

45

Unchained and Free to Become!

"For he who has died has been freed from sin. Now if we died with Christ, we believe that we shall also live with Him, knowing that Christ, having been raised from the dead, dies no more. Death no longer has dominion over Him. For the death that He died, He died to sin once for all; but the life that He lives, He lives to God. Likewise, you also reckon yourselves to be dead indeed to sin, but alive to God in Christ Jesus our Lord." (Romans 6:11-17)

The miracle of the new birth must be one of the most liberating experiences that an individual can go through this side of eternity! When a man has been bound by the chains of the flesh, the world, and the devil's lies, he lives a life far from God's purpose and destiny for him or her. As a matter of fact, there is nothing a man can do (in his own power) to help his situation since he was born damned!

Listen to this factual statement delivered by the Apostle John in 1 John 3:8: "The Son of God appeared for this purpose, to destroy the works of the devil." Does this Scripture fill you with hope? Do you understand the promise, the power, and the purpose of these words? Jesus came to destroy everything the devil has released upon humanity since the fall of Adam. He came to set humanity free so they can become all that God intended for them to be and to have.

Freedom in Christ

Without the cleansing blood of Jesus from sin and the repositioning or alignment with God, man is doomed and headed for a Christ-less eternity. Only the blood of Jesus can align you with God the Father and bring you into favor with God. Once aligned, your freedom begins to manifest itself in many ways. Let me share a few places where alignment is gained...

- **Mind.** Our mind, which was once marred, indifferent, and in opposition to God's mind, is the first thing touched by the blood of Jesus. The realization that you don't have the power to change yourself is truly the beginning of wisdom. Once a man "gets it," and that person realizes that without God's leadership in his life he is lost, God can start a transformational work. By agreeing with God that you, as a human, can't change your life by your own power and by accepting Him into your heart as the new leader within you, you will experience an awakening.

- **Heart.** Our hearts carry all our emotions. Our hearts were initially made to feel and experience God's emotions. A heart that is consumed with self can only hurt and be hurt. Once the heart has been washed by the blood of Jesus, it will experience the amazing, unending love of God. It is this emotion, along with a renewed mind, that causes an individual to express heartfelt worship and service to God.

- **Hands & Feet.** Once your mind is renewed and your heart is filled with God's love, a desire to do the same for others will follow. Obedience then becomes possible as you seek to do God's will. In fact, serving Jesus is not only a healthy challenge but also a requirement. To stay free from sin, you must keep pressing in and pursue God's will. Ignoring the God-given desires now burning in your heart is setting yourself up for failure.

Remember, we have been set free by the power of Jesus' blood; free to love and serve the King of kings! Since we have been raised from a life of corruption and sin, we are now alive to pursue all that God has prepared for us! Neh'enah.

46

Too Much of Me!

"But let a man examine himself, and so let him eat of the bread and drink of the cup." (1 Corinthians 11:28)

When the time for communion, or what others call the Lord's Supper, comes around in your church, there is usually a presentation of the emblems and an explanation of the juice and the bread. After the minister prays over the elements, most people will go to the front to partake of the emblems. This is typically a time for deep spiritual reflection.

I believe that taking the Lord's Supper daily is a good practice. A regular time to evaluate and search the heart—in my humble opinion—is often beneficial, not just once a month.

Examination Time!

One thing I have noticed about the religious people in our churches, yes, the modern-day Pharisee— you know him or her— they sit in the church pews, with no intention of ever stepping out of the boat with the boldness to walk on water. These will always be quick to judge the spiritual condition of others but never their own! Have you met such people? If you haven't, you will soon!

Paul said, **"But let a man examine himself..."** For starters, what does the word examine mean? The word "examine" comes from the word "watching." It is used for both a person and an object. To examine then means to "test in battle," "reliable," or "trustworthy." It also refers to a person who is tested, significant, recognized, esteemed, or worthy. Additionally, it means "tested to see if it's valuable."

The process of examining the heart begins with our willingness to let the Holy Spirit have His gentle way within us. He must be granted permission to move through the corridors of our heart and search to see if there is anything in us that is not worthy, reliable, or valuable.

Nothing Started Happening in Me Until I Stopped Lying to Myself!

I once heard a man say this, and I'm quoting him: "Nothing started happening in me until I stopped lying to myself."

Many people know God's personal will for us. God hasn't hidden His perfect will from you or me; in fact, He revealed it many years ago. The real problem is that we haven't embraced His will for our lives. When it involves faith, sacrifice, or stepping out, we tend to dismiss it from our minds and hearts. We've convinced ourselves that we can do just fine without God's perfect will. I'm not sharing this so someone will agree or disagree; I'm simply making a general observation.

God has given His creation the power to inherit the earth; therefore, man does not align himself with God's agenda.

Here is my conclusion on this matter: God speaks to man's heart. He reveals His will. Man should run with God's command and follow through. Why don't we do it? What holds us back? Circumstances? Situations? Timing? The main issue is that too much of ourselves, too much of what we want [not what God wants], blocks the flow of what God intends to do in us and through us.

Until we can genuinely point the finger at ourselves and carefully examine our hearts, then and only then can we progress in our God-given mission. Neh'enah.

47

Did You Forget What You Prayed For?

"Our God shall come and shall not keep silent.
A fire shall devour before Him,
And it shall be very tempestuous all around Him." (Psalm 50:3)

I often come across believers and servants of the Lord facing numerous tests and trials in their lives. "How can this be?" they ask. "Why are all these things happening to me in such a short time?" "I am going through 'hell,' and I don't understand why!"

If you have been involved with the Christian faith for a while, you have probably encountered some well-meaning, faithful, and humble servants who have been tested beyond measure. Sometimes, there are no words of encouragement to offer them; all you can do is pray for their situation and ask that God would help them press through.

It's a God Response.

Here's something I've learned through my walk with Jesus over the years. Because not everyone responds the same way to God and not all have ears to hear what the Spirit is saying, those who do often face the "floods" of tests.

When an immature believer witnesses a more mature believer going through a crisis, they are often confused by the struggles the mature believer faces. They ask the mature believer, "Why are you going through this? Aren't you supposed to know God?" "I thought you had a handle on all this?" and so on.

What the immature believer doesn't realize is that one day, he will mature; and it will be then, at that moment, that he will go through his own furnace and brokenness. Immature believers don't face God's fiery furnace until God knows they are ready to handle it.

But returning to your own fiery furnace, many of the crises and struggles that mature believers face are related to a response from the Lord. You see, it could be that after many days, weeks, or even years, the believer has prayed to God, saying, "Jesus, I want to know You more deeply!" or "Lord, let me experience the fellowship of Your sufferings!" or "I want more of Your fire in me!" Your testing, your crisis, your adversity—it's all an answer to your heartfelt prayer for more of Jesus in you! Do you understand this?

It is Tempestuous All Around Him!

In Psalm 50:3, the Word describes a storm that surrounds the Lord. It is only natural that if you are moving closer to Him, you will first have to face the storm. Does this make sense to you? I sincerely pray it does.

You see, a man or a woman of God who desires more of Jesus's nature within them will only achieve this by coming into oneness with the Lord. One must enter the Lord to be like the Lord—in mind, in thought, in nature, in mindset, in wisdom, and in all things!

What is a Tempest?

A tempest in the Hebrew word used here means something turbulent or stormy. When you are drawing near to His heart, you will experience His fire, turbulence, and it will become very stormy. This is how you know that you are drawing near His heart.

The next time you call upon the Lord and make your petition known, expect Him to answer you. When you ask Him to draw you close, then anticipate fire and tumultuous experiences to come your way. Not because God is trying to destroy you; He is simply drawing you nearer to His heart! Neh'enah.

48

Deserts! Part 1

"I cared for you in the wilderness, in the land of drought." (Hosea 13:5)

Every believer I have met during my short walk in the kingdom of God can all testify that going through "desert-like" experiences is part of walking with God.

Deserts in the Scriptures almost always symbolize a time of breaking and humility—a period of testing and personal challenges, especially in character.

Though we understand that deserts are part of living in the kingdom of God, we need to also ask ourselves the question "why" am I being placed in a desert?

Here is what I believe the Lord shared with me this past week regarding deserts.

The Lord showed me three reasons for deserts in our lives. Some deserts come because of disobedience; others happen because of our hunger and thirst after God; and finally, some deserts occur as part of God's preparation of the vessel.

I want to analyze these more thoroughly.

The Desert of Disobedience

"Cursed is the man who trusts in man
And makes flesh his strength,

Whose heart departs from the LORD.
For he shall be like a shrub in the desert,
And shall not see when good comes,
But shall inhabit the parched places in the wilderness,
In a salt land which is not inhabited." (Jeremiah 17:5, 6)

Disobedience begins when we make our **"flesh our strength."** The second we start to put our trust in flesh is the moment our hearts will turn away from the Lord. The result of this is that we will end up like a shrub in the desert. We will live in parched places in the wilderness, in a salt land that is not inhabited.

Often, when we, as children of God, go through desert-like experiences, we tend not to want to be held responsible for what's happening to us. We quickly find ways to escape by blaming others, our circumstances, or other factors.

There are even certain brothers and sisters who make a feeble attempt at rebuking spirits and demons out of the "rebellious." The Scripture says, "God setteth the solitary in families: he bringeth out those which are bound with chains: but the rebellious dwell in a dry land." (Psalm 68:6)

The rebellious remain on dry land because that's where their hearts are—dry. And that's a choice!

As I conclude this first part of your meditation, identify anything in your life that you know is disobedience to God's voice. Once you recognize it, repent. Avoid blaming others for your bad luck, misfortunes, and mishaps.

If you find yourself in a desert, start by checking your heart; if there is no sin within you, then you will recognize that God is at work in your life. If you do have sin, then you need to repent and return to a land full of blessing. Neh'enah.

49

Deserts! Part 2

"Then Jesus was led up by the Spirit into the wilderness to be tempted by the devil." (Matthew 4:1)

Deserts for Those Being Prepared for Service

Even though many situations lead us into arid, desert-like places due to disobedience to God's voice, not all desert experiences are caused by disobedience. As I mentioned in my last blog, sometimes God will lead us into desert-like times because of obedience.

I understand that many believers in the body of Christ today aren't fond of topics like repentance, brokenness, and having a submissive heart to God; however, it's essential to embrace these. It's crucial that we learn to walk in everything God has graciously prepared for us.

Now, let's move on to the topic above.

Here is an interesting fact that happened in the very life of the Son of God, in the life of Jesus Christ Himself.

The Scripture says that Jesus Himself was led by the Spirit into the wilderness. When we read this story, we might question it a bit. The Scripture states that the Spirit led Jesus into the wilderness. It wasn't Christ's idea to go into the wilderness; it was God's plan! Do you see this?

Sometimes, our obedience requires us to venture into the wilderness for necessary breaking and refining. The lessons learned in a desert-like experience are unmatched! I don't believe anyone is genuinely asking for this, but God sees it from His perspective.

I don't believe God takes His servants into the wilderness without knowing that His servant is fully capable of overcoming it. Often, the Lord will lead His servants into the wilderness to test them, to prepare them, and to empower them for ministry.

Unique Tests Happen in the Wilderness

I have often thought in my quiet times, "Jesus could have been tested by the Father at a different location or in a different setting. He could have - but He didn't! He chose a desert, a wilderness!"

My dear friends, does this make you wonder why?

Here's my answer: Because in a desert-like experience, you find nothing fleshly to hold on to. There are no friends there, no gadgets or gimmicks there, and nothing emotional to cling to—that's why. It's just you and God!

A test in the wilderness will figuratively 'squeeze out the honey' from you. It will push you to dig deep for meaning. Your resolve will be tested. Will you persevere; will you grow weary?

I believe that nothing will test you more thoroughly and deeply than spending quality time in the wilderness where God has placed you.

Remember, it was the Spirit that led Jesus into the wilderness to be tested, not the devil! Neh'enah.

50

Deserts! Part 3

A Psalm of David When He Was in the Wilderness of Judah.

"O God, You are my God;
Early will I seek You;
My soul thirsts for You;
My flesh longs for You
In a dry and thirsty land
Where there is no water.
So I have looked for You in the sanctuary,
To see Your power and Your glory." (Psalm 63:1-2)

Deserts for Those Who Hunger and Thirst for More of God

In this third part of my short series on deserts, I want to highlight the experience that David, the man of God, went through.

After David's son, Absalom, revolted against his father, David and his men fled Jerusalem and took the Jericho Road through the northern part of the wilderness of Judah. It was here that David made his prayer known.

There are a couple of things we can learn from this revelation: The first is that when we face pressure, we tend to worry rather than worship; we tend to run instead of rest, and we tend to try instead of trust. When external forces crowd our lives, we end up pushing God's presence out.

The second thing we can learn is that deserts can make us very thirsty. Whether it is a natural or spiritual experience, deserts will have that effect on us.

I believe that often God brings things or circumstances into our lives to push us out of our comfort zones. It is necessary. As things start to move all around us, we need to act and handle the issue at hand. It doesn't matter how difficult or easy it is, we must address it.

When we encounter a desert-like experience, we will do one of two things: either complain and whine about the adversity or open our hearts to the Holy Spirit and say, "Give me more of Jesus!" Neh'enah.

51

Owner of a Stubborn Heart!

"But My people would not heed My voice and Israel would have none of Me.
So I gave them over to their own stubborn heart, to walk in their own counsels.
"Oh, that My people would listen to Me, that Israel would walk in My ways!
I would soon subdue their enemies and turn My hand against their adversaries."
(Psalm 81:11-14)

When a servant of the Lord deepens their relationship with Him, they start to understand what the Lord expects from them and what He does not want.

God's servants, those who pursue a closer relationship with God, always desire the Father's heart. It is in their nature to want all that God has for them!

At the same time, we have servants who operate on a different, more compromising level. They take a little of what they want and a little of what God truly desires. These dear servants are the ones I want to draw your attention to—those who won't let go of the little foxes that spoil their vine.

Jehovah God had a huge following—probably over two million Hebrew children, who followed Moses out of Egypt. Some followed sincerely after God, while others followed for convenience; still, others followed with a mixed heart.

Now, please understand that the call to holiness is a call that says, "God is first and His Holy Spirit must first inspect everything I want or desire!"

Once God approves something in your life, you can move forward. These are great times for experiencing God's blessing. However, there are other times when God doesn't approve and makes it known to you through His Holy Spirit.

The Real Challenge Starts Here

The real test for all believers begins when God says "no" to you on any matter. Will we obey or rebel? The choice is ours!

If one understands why God says "no," then this man or woman will be walking in brokenness. If the individual persists in being stubborn with God, there will come a time when God lets that servant have his own way. God will turn him over to their own desires. In essence, God is saying, "If you want your toy, you can have it - but it will cost you in the end!"

It's Like Climbing a Mountain

Once a man decides to do whatever he wants without caring about God, he begins an uphill climb in living his life before God.

Everything will become a challenge. Things won't come easily for you anymore. It will almost feel like God is no longer working with you—but against you. The emotional effort of convincing yourself that "God is still with you" will drain you.

Every wrong thing that happens to you will seem like a conspiracy designed to bring you down. It is a horrible sinking feeling. Nothing will change until you realize that you have been stubborn against the Holy Spirit.

God Will Subdue Your Enemies

If you are living in outward rebellion against the Holy Spirit, the enemy has every right to rise against you. If there is no sin in your life, then clearly, the enemy is trying to bring you down. At this point, you can rebuke and free yourself from the lies and strategies the devil has set against you. But first, check your heart to see if you are walking under God's authority and guidance.

If everything is right between you and God, then rejoice in the Lord, for **"the God of peace shall soon crush Satan under your feet."** (Romans 16:20) Neh'enah.

52

Are You Up for Promotion Yet?

"Moreover, it is required in stewards that one be found faithful." (1 Corinthians 4:2)

As I meditated on this one verse, the Holy Spirit started sharing His heart with me about promotion and future opportunities.

Is it any wonder why some people always get the best opportunities in life while others never seem to catch a break? Is there a genuine reason for this? Maybe there is a "science" behind it!

I am not really sure if there is a genuine reason or a science to this, but here is what I know – If one is faithful or shows himself faithful with what he or she has at hand, all sorts of promotions will not be far. This much I know!

When a door of opportunity opens in your life, always remember, it is an opportunity for you to express yourself and do all you can with it; an opportunity is NOT about what the open door can do for you, but what it will do IN you.

So, here are some things we are handed down to prove ourselves faithful:

Faithful in Instruction. We often receive instruction, whether at work or in life, and we are immediately tested on it. The real issue is whether we follow through with what we have been taught, shown, or challenged with. If we prove ourselves to be good stewards of instruction, we will receive more.

Faithful in Responsibility. When I think of responsibility, I always remember my old boss at one of my secular jobs. I remember this lesson as if it were yesterday, but it's been more than thirty years ago, to be exact.

At this job, it seemed like I was always the one chosen to do or handle things. My boss usually picked me over my coworkers, and honestly, I never knew why.

One day, one of my coworkers said to me, "Why are they working you so much? It isn't fair. Don't let them do this to you!" "If I were you," he added, "I would complain to the head office that you are getting overworked and severely underpaid!" This planted a thought in my head, but it was not a good one!

I notice myself becoming a bit rebellious toward authority and defiant of the protocol at work. One day, I finally did it. My boss called me for a special assignment, and I replied, "Am I the only person who works here?!" I said these words with a bad attitude. My boss called me into the office and said, "David, are you paying for a car? A mortgage?" To which I replied, "Of course!" Then my boss suggested, "Well, if you have debt, I suggest that you do what you are told here at work... unless you want to be without a job." It doesn't take a rocket scientist to understand these words. I responded, "Yes, sir!"

After "clearing the air" a bit with my boss, I walked out of the office with a strong sense of conviction. I felt terrible! Plus, I was confused about why I was acting the way I was. I love God, but a thought that wasn't from Him had entered my mind! It came from someone who doesn't know or follow God's ways. I allowed it to influence my heart and mind.

After getting home that afternoon, I spent some time in prayer. I repented of my actions, words, and attitude. I told God I was sorry for the way I had been acting, and He heard my cry from His holy hill and cleansed me with His precious blood. I told the Lord that I wanted to be a faithful servant with my life, not a stumbling block to anyone. I know God heard me.

The next day, I apologized to my boss and said, "You will never see that old rebellious David again!" My boss then told me, "I have had my eyes on you. I'm preparing you for promotion. That is why I always pick on you!"

My friend, stay faithful wherever God has placed you. You might not en-joy what you face every day, but remember, God has chosen you to share in His suffering. If you stay faithful, you'll be on your way to greatness! Neh'enah.

For more books written by David Mayorga,

please visit:

www.shabarpublications.com

www.ingramcontent.com/pod-product-compliance
Lightning Source LLC
Chambersburg PA
CBHW021828090426
42811CB00032B/2067/J